Why Won't
My Buddy
Get Up . . .

13037-OGEE

Why Won't
My Buddy
Get Up . . .

Douglas Garrett O'Geen

3037-OGEE

To order additional copies of this book, contact:
Xlibris Corporation
1-888-7-XLIBRIS
www.Xlibris.com
Orders@Xlibris.com

I would like to make a dedication without stating names, which would ruin the only surprise element of the novel. Therefore, I dedicate this book to the family who has hurt the most from the sad occurrence, as well as to the young man who has suffered even more . . . my buddy.

Chapter One

I was stuck in that daydream trance again. Most of the lights in the room were turned off. The only one on was a dim desk lamp. Yet it was bright enough to reveal that horrible picture.

It was clearly visible—pinned up with that black tack onto the bulletin board that came with the desk. The bulletin board had been cheaply built. The metal lining on the outside was tearing apart. The screws had practically fallen out so that the only thing holding the flimsy board in place was the Elmer's Superglue that someone had applied probably three years earlier.

The board was just like his family—or at least it seemed that way. They were just tearing apart at the seams with only a smidgen of hope for recovering. They held that hope and would live or die with that belief grasped strongly between the aging knuckles of their fingers.

My desk lamp lit the picture, and everything else around it was black. My lamp was like a spotlight on the picture. It was the spotlight that he would have been in this year—for cross-country, for basketball, and for baseball. It was his #35 that would have been out there in front of a sold-out crowd, with every one of them cheering him on in that "oh-so-important game." He would've shot the three-pointer. The kid had the strangest posture, but he could cash everything.

He was so gawky, tall and skinny-like. He'd stop dead one inch before the three-point circle—it looked almost like he was going to fall over a cliff and that he stopped just in time before falling. He would then regain form and grab that big orange ball with his big skinny hands, and start from his lower right hip and bring it all the way up his body, above his head until he finally released the ball. The ball would spin so much I swear I could see the air struggle to move out of the way. The kid wouldn't miss if he shot the ball blindfolded. Then there was the sound of the net. The rippling sound of that oversized spinning orange hitting and touching every part of that tightly bound thread. The net seemed like it wanted to keep that ball forever; to hold its new baby in its womb for as long as possible. Then the roaring cheers would come and the net would let its little child go, so that it could experience life and the treacherous Earth.

Notice how the ball hits the ground. It fights hard to stay in that security net, but it has no choice but to fall free. It knows it's going down and that when it hits bottom, there will be nothing but pain. The ball has no power to stop that fall. It has a fate and follows through with it because it has no other choice. It then flexes up and crashes to the ground. The ground is its downfall, the lowest point in its life. It meets the dirt and dust that comes off every basketball player's stylish sneakers, and then fights to get away. It stays there for the shortest possible time and then bounces back up, hoping to escape fate forever; though it knows fate will once again capture it, and its history will repeat over and over again.

A sweat droplet formed on the right side of my head as I thought about this. It flowed down my face until it met my right eyebrow, and then became tangled up in the silent brown guards. It struggled to get through, but didn't have enough strength. It kept struggling anyway.

My sweat droplet struggled as I struggled to hold back my tears. The last time I cried was when I was twelve years old. I couldn't do it now. I've always felt that a grown mans' tears were a sign of weakness. Those tears flowing down your face indicate that you're helpless to a situation. It means that something has gotten the best of you—and in a world like this, it is dangerous to let any situation become overpowering. And I'd be pissed if I let that saltwater mixture fall from my eye, allowing it to make its way down my face, leaving a clear, wet trail behind it. You could wipe the trail away; but the fact is, it was still there. After all, the past cannot be changed. I don't care if I'm the only one who knows it was there. I'm out to prove something to myself, not to anybody else. If I prove to myself that I am weak, then I've just disappointed one of the most important people in my life.

I hated looking at that picture. It made me despondent, yet I felt anger at the same time. I felt rage beginning in my heart. It was growing in that red garden of mine—not a garden of food, but a garden of feelings and emotions. It was where my emotions began, and where they persisted. And that is where my rage was planted and where it continues to grow. Once the rage gets too large for that garden, it runs into my veins . . . taking up ever more space until it controls me—making me want to punch something . . . anything! I wanted to roar like the strongest lion, to throw my arm into a violent whirlwind and punch through a brick wall to feel the severing pain in my cracked-up, bloody knuckles. Then feel that pain find its way up my whole arm and crawl through my elbow while adding salt to my every wound. I then wanted to pull my arm back and get ready for another chance to make my arm a pulsating piece of dying equipment. I would have loved to do this steadily, and then stand back and eye those bricks until they melted under my burning retina.

My brown eyes darkened with rage and my face was hardened into a fiery stone of Mt. Rushmore. My once smooth and methodical breathing suddenly became erratic and heavy, with more oxygen leaving upon exhalation rather than entering my suffocating lungs. I noticed my hands had clenched up into fists and my back had straightened up stiffly against my padded chair.

Tap tap tap . . . tap tap tap . . . tap tap tap tap tap tap tap tap . . ."Shit!" That's all I could say in my panicking state of mind. My eyes bulged out and my body loosened up instantaneously. I took a deep breath of air to catch up for all the lost oxygen during my state of rage.

"Uh . . . uh . . . Heather, I'm masturbating. You'll have to hold on."

I knew who it was by the knock that she used. It was a sort of understood Morse code between our little clique of friends. I never really made a knock for myself. I just pounded on the door, and all my college buddies knew that it was me.

"Ha, ha Doug. You would think you get enough of that from Bowman's mother."

Bowman was my roommate. He was a good friend in high school so we roomed together at college. He was a cool kid and picked up some pretty girlfriends in his lifetime. He was no Don Juan, but he came up with some very sly pick up lines. The kid wore glasses and his hair was sticking up in the back or on the side probably twenty hours a day. He wasn't out there to impress people so he only brushed his hair when he wanted to. But anyway, we always have and will pick on each other's mothers. We even wrote poems and stories to each other on e-mail and then sent them to all our friends to get other people involved in the whole criticism barrage. I just chuckled to myself after Heather made that comment because I realized how much it was working.

I regained composure and walked over to the door to open the creaking wood slowly.

"What's up Heather? I see that ya miss me already."

"Oh yes Doug. I thought I'd come back for a second orgasm seeing that you're Mr. Bombastic and all. I gathered up just enough strength for you to work your magic."

Her tone was quite sarcastic and to say the truth, I didn't like it too awfully much. She'd be lucky to have my ten-foot pole anywhere near her. Thinking of this only made me think of him again. I unwillingly glanced across the picture on my bulletin board, causing my blood to rush carelessly through my veins. It made me think of him because it was one of his favorite sayings, "I wouldn't touch her with my ten-foot dick pole," as opposed to the saying that most people use. But I realized that I would be showing my feelings and I quickly changed my mood into a fake laugh.

I'm the type of person who doesn't like to admit that occurrences like this bother me. It's not really a front. It's just that I hear girls like Heather complain about foolish things. And it's foolish things like a guy she likes that doesn't like her. Or one of the lust men (term the college girls use for a guy they're obtrusively lusting over) already has a girlfriend.

I think it's pathetic to make a little problem into an ulcer. But she's had her problems in the past, which is also why I didn't want to tell her about my buddy. She once had a boyfriend whom she was in love with die in a fatal car crash three days before his graduation from high school. There were two other guys in the car and they somehow survived, but her boyfriend did not.

I just knew if I told her about my buddy, then she would say, "Well, at least he's not dead," or, "Look at what I had to deal with." I hate hearing that nonsense. People didn't know my buddy and they don't truly know me. I feel bad that other people have to go through that, but my problem is my problem and theirs are theirs. So I don't want anybody telling me that they had it worse. First of all, I'm aware of the fact that God has given me a good life. I've never denied that. So in my own opinion, when people make such statements, I feel it is one of the most selfish phrases that any human can utter.

I stood up and after stretching my joints to the sky; I walked over to the miniature fridge that I had rented for the year. It was quite the junky fridge, but the poster on the front made it all worthwhile. It was of this beautiful woman lifting up her shirt just enough so that you could see the bottom of her perfectly rounded breasts. Then, to the right, it had a perfect saying to match. "Take two of these and call me in the morning." I'll take two of those I thought, but I wouldn't be calling her the next morning. It would be the next night when I could go for another round of my medication.

I was finally able to pry my eyes off the picture, just long enough to open the fridge and grab myself a beer. Heather, who had found her way onto my bed, broke out in a chuckle. "What are ya laughing at you hyena?"

"I see you looking at that girl . . ." She began to chuckle again and had difficulty saying what she wanted to in between all her giggling. "And . . . ha, ha, ha . . . and the only way you could ever get a woman like that is in your dreams . . . ha, ha, ha, ha, ha . . ." She just broke out into hysterical laughter at her sorry excuse for a joke. I just stared at her in amazement and wondered to myself, how could anybody laugh at such an ignorant comment?

But even though the insult was petty, I still had to come back with a sarcastic remark. "Kind of makes ya jealous that you aren't the woman in that dream, ha?"

She just put on that look. She had this look that spoke for itself: "Now that was just plain rude." As if I cared. I bet she wanted me, so she had no right to make a comment like that. So I just kept on with the snide remarks.

"I bet you wish you had breasts that were perfectly round too . . . hell, you probably wish I would . . ."

"All right, that's enough Doug!" She stood up and pranced over to me looking for a fight. We always fought, just playing around of course. She would start hitting me on the arm. I would try to stay calm as long as possible, but always lost control quickly. I would grab onto her, put her in a headlock, twist my body around for more power, and then burst out with energy—heaving her onto my bed. I would then jump on top of her, shake the bed so that it would make an old, creaking sound, all the while scream-ing—"Who's yo Daddy? Who's yo Daddy?"—just to make it sound like we were having sex. After boring with that, I would pounce on her leg, starting from the top of her hip and proceeding all the way down her calf. Sometimes I even left bruises that her father would see. He probably thought I was a woman beater, but that didn't concern me. The fact was she just bruised easily. Time heals all wounds, so these ones always healed just in time for us to get into another fight, so that I could batter her up some more.

So the fight was like all the rest of our fun, little quarrels. After we finished, I staggered back to my chair and took a deep breath after my hard-fought battle. I looked over at her and she put on a pout. "You're so mean to me." She then buried her head deep into my pillow, putting on a pitiful act of being depressed.

I just laughed and rested my physically drained body into my chair. I grabbed my beer off my desk and clenched it tightly in my palm as if it were a prisoner with no chance of escaping me. I then looked over to the picture, wrinkled up my face into an angry grimace, and tilted the bottle fiercely up to my mouth— pouring it like there was a time limit on it, and swallowing it until every last drop went into my thirsting mouth.

Heather stood up about five minutes later, trampled out hoping that I would notice and possibly stop her. But I didn't acknowledge her. I didn't move. I just zoned in on that picture on my desk until my body made a startled jump when I heard the door slam shut behind me. But my eyes remained in the same place and my vision became blurry, sending me into my own world where I could watch the television of my imagination, the place that sent me back into my past and fantasizing about the future. And it was that world in which I was captured.

Chapter Two

We walked a little closer, being careful with every step we took. It was our E.B. gang and we had to use caution so we wouldn't get caught. East Bethany was the little town that my little clan of friends was from. We always caused havoc on that town, causing the police to come down and secure the place every weekend due to angry town folk complaining about too much noise or about 'someone' sneaking around their house late at night. We hadn't been caught yet and we had to keep the successive streak going.

The night air was misty, a light fog overseeing the tops of the tallest trees. The sky was dark without a cloud in sight. The only guiding light for us was a few stars and a tiny crack of a moon that was showing.

I took one more step, inching myself closer to that large building called Kistner Concrete. Many of our gangs' adventures stemmed from this construction site. We liked to razz the fellas who worked there and try and get as close as possible to them without getting caught. So I stepped another inch closer, causing myself to step on a jagged rock. A slight grimace of pain expressed itself across my face. But I let the grimace go once I stared at the land full of multi-ton blocks of concrete. I thought how much it would hurt if I was caught beneath that, and I thought about how if rocks could feel pain, then the rock that I had stepped on already knew the feeling.

"Should we sneak in, Jeff?" A solemn expression scrawled over my face as I waited for a reply.

"I don't know, why don't you decide?" A slight pause followed, until it was interrupted by an outburst of laughter from Damian. He quickly added a comment, adjoining it with his laughter.

"You two are worried about getting caught by a couple of blue-collar construction lugs ... ha, ha, what do they do for a living? Seriously, they work on concrete blocks. They work on something that their own head is probably made out of. All they ..."

My mind started wandering as he babbled on and on. First of all, I couldn't stand to listen to his voice when he complained. It was so whiny and girlish, almost nasal sounding. I thought maybe a little fairy girl had jumped into his air passages, stolen his voice box, and was speaking for him. He was the hippie type brought back from the sixties. He always wore Salvation Army clothes that cost him no more than two dollars, and an orange leather jacket from the seventies. It fit tightly to his body, making him look like more of a wimp than he already was.

" ... And then you act all tough and tell me that nobody's gonna catch you. No, not you guys. You seem to have this big plan of harassing these guys, yet you're too scared t—"

"Would you shut up, Rat Teeth?!" I stared into his eyes with a killer's rage. Rat Teeth was one of the famous nicknames that our E.B. gang used for him. His teeth were spread out and they stuck out like a rat's, thus earning the name. He always said how he planned to get braces but couldn't because his mom was too poor. I believed him. The kid had it pretty tough. He had to buy everything for himself, which is probably one of the reasons why he got into the grungy style of clothes ... because he couldn't afford anything else.

I bent down to pick up a handful of rocks, then used my hand as a strainer to let go of the tiny excess rocks, leaving me with three baseball sized ones in my hand. I then fired one of them onto the roof of the concrete target. A sharp sounding clang was heard with very little echo to it. "What a pitiful throw that was." I had to whisper it, trying to be as secretive as possible.

I then threw my second rock and waited for a reply from my newfound inorganic friend. It replied with a hit to the ground and a splash in a little puddle. Jeff whispered behind me, "That was worse than the last one," and then whispered a chuckle that sounded more like an echo of the rocks.

I turned around with a grin and nodded my head in agreement. "What do you say we go in?" I tried to make myself appear brave by displaying a cocky smile. Truthfully, I was trembling with fear.

Jeff had quite a simple comeback. "I don't know, throw another rock."

I just looked at Jeff. "Is that your big solution?" My head began to nod side to side in disbelief, implying that his answer was completely ridiculous. "Just keep throwing rocks until maybe we're heard, is that right?"

Jeff's reply was once again so simple. "Yeah, that's what I said."

A small burst of air was then let out of my nostrils, a somewhat snorting laugh that resulted in a snotty tone. I then transferred my third rock from my left to my right hand and, annoyed, I swung back and hurled the rock into the air with all my nine years worth of baseball experience behind me. We stood there waiting for another reply for only a few seconds, though it seemed like hours. The rock hit a large metal support block, sending the loudest clang of vibration throughout the small town of East Bethany. All three of us stood there for a few seconds, like we were prepared to attack any enemy that might arise.

An ignition was then heard turning over in the bushes to the right of us, and two tiny, bright moons cast out, forming our silhouettes on a trashy junk pile of cars behind us. Realizing it was probably a night watchman from Kistner, I stood planted there.

Frozen in the imprints that my shoes had made, I wondered if I would finally get caught.

"Shit!" Jeff once again made this simple comment, which this time seemed to fit perfectly into the mold of what I was thinking. "Let's get the hell outta here!"

I looked to Jeff and watched him pick up his borrowed bike, and spring himself up over the top almost like he had been reincarnated from the Civil War cavalry division. Because it seemed like the only plan we had to avoid being arrested, I followed Jeff's idea, and grabbed hold of my fairly new twelve-speeded Schwinn bike. I once again used my baseball experience and tossed the bike over my shoulder and into a straight up position, setting it on the ground before me. As I jumped onto the bike seat, I felt an uncomfortable pain in my testicles from the impact of hitting the seat. But with virtually no time to worry about it, I tore through the rocky road, following my trusty friend Jeff. The car gave chase behind us and it didn't take long for us to pass Damian, who must have taken off before Jeff and I. But sadly enough, that slight lead wasn't even close to enough. He probably would have been better off running. He owned one of those one-speed Huffy bikes that you sell at a garage sale when you're ten years old. It was the *only* bike he owned. To make matters even worse, he also had a flat tire on the back, so his unfortunate lack of money was causing another unsolved problem. But there was little time to worry about him. We would help him in any way that we could, but at the moment, we were all looking for some sort of safe haven.

I kept following Jeff's path, because I myself had no idea how to escape from the seemingly disgruntled worker. An eerie feeling passed through my veins, yet at the same time, a nervous excitement. So I just kept following Jeff, a leader at heart, but never being boastful about it.

He made a quick turn onto some bumpy path to our right. This path was behind the old-fashioned style General Store, owned by Damian's mother. It was their only source of income and also a good source of beer for us under-agers. The path we turned onto led straight to the middle of Kistner Concrete, so I was skeptical at first to follow him. But I had little time, and pretty much no choice, so I followed on just hoping that he had some detailed plan mapped into his brain.

I turned my head to the side, looking for Damian. He was still on the trail that we had just turned off of, sweat pouring down his cheeks and a look of terror on his face. The car was about two feet behind him, many times idling the engine down and applying the brakes to avoid rear ending and killing the poor kid. We wanted to help him, but we could do nothing at that moment with Jeff and I being helpless ourselves.

I turned my head forward, eyeing Jeff's back and just praying that he wasn't leading us into a trap. My prayers were quickly answered, as his next strategic move was a sharp turn onto a steep, grassy hill—which would bring us around to the side of the brick store. It was very bumpy, forcing my front tire to the left and my back tire the opposite. But I gained control and kept pedaling hard toward the top of the hill, getting all my strength from adrenaline alone. I watched as Jeff navigated his bike onto level ground at the top of the hill, then I followed his trail and also reached that destination. We both simultaneously applied our brakes, which sent our tires into a controlled skid and caused a cloud of dust to arise behind us that hid us for a couple millionths of a second.

"What should we do with our bikes?!" My voice was no longer concealing my fear. My fear was revealed with every trembling word I spoke.

"Uh . . . just throw 'em in the trees to hide 'em. He won't know we're here then." His voice was also shaky, helping me to realize that I was not alone in my panic.

The car could be heard sliding on the rocky trail that we had just left, so we knew we didn't have much time before he would pass us. We both picked up our bikes in unison and tossed them into the evergreen trees in front of us. We jumped in directly behind the bikes, feeling the prickly pine needles poking against our skin. Normally I would have been screaming in agony. But the adrenaline was a blessing, making the agonizing pain a minute problem in our quest to escape.

Jeff and I sat there stiffly between those trees. The only sounds heard echoing through the night air was our rhythmic breathing, a scattered muffler, and a rusted engine that was practically held together by duct tape. I could swear the car would quit any second. If I was gambling, I would have bet my hard earned savings on it; although it was probably a good thing I didn't. The car never did quit. It was like a sequel to Steven Spielberg's movie, *Christine*. I was only hoping that this car wasn't going to chase us 'til we were so fatigued that we would just lie down and wait for certain death, as the one in the movie did.

The car sped past, traveling on the rocky road behind the store. We realized that it was probably chasing Damian, but were held there fairly powerless to do anything to help him. We just had to wait and see what would happen and hope that he would use some sort of alien intelligence to figure out a scheme.

Noticing that it was safe to whisper, I let some hoarse words slip from my mouth. "Dude man . . . I gotta admit, I'm kinda scared. If any of us get caught, we're all goin' down."

Jeff knew exactly what I meant and nodded his head in nervous agreement while letting out his response. "No shit, me too!" His eyes looked wider and his legs were tensed so that if we did get spotted, he could spring forward and make a break for freedom. I also got into position, almost expecting another crazy chance at a mad dash, but not wanting it.

Perspiration began to build up on my face, helped along by the dew in the misty air. We heard the screeching and rolling of tires going back and forth on the rocky road. After much trial and error, he hydroplaned on the rocks and managed to turn around the side of the store opposite from us. This led to the main road. He took a right there and squealed his tires, venting his frustration and making his way toward Pavilion, another small town.

Jeff and I both watched as the car struggled to make its way toward its destination. We stayed in that slightly bent position and watched the brake lights pass over a small hill and out of view. We were not yet ready to come out, afraid that maybe something or somebody was still waiting for us. It was one of those feelings where you're in a war, hiding from the enemy. You stay in that hidden area, sheltering yourself from danger until you're assured of security. Because once you stick your head up into view, the enemy will begin target practice on your candy filled brain as if it was a piñata.

Crackling stones were heard under a 171-pound frame, and then that whiny voice saying, "Hey guys, where are you?"

A wide smile and a couple "ha, haaaaaaaaaaah's" blurted out my mouth. Jeff jumped out of the bushes and slapped Damian on the shoulder, greeting him with a "How'd you pull that one off you big stud?!"

Damian shook his head as he tried to regain his breath. I stared into his eyes and could see the look of terror, which was most likely implanted there for the rest of the night. After successfully gathering an ounce of oxygen from the atmosphere, he began his story taking a deep breath after each word. "Construction . . . boy . . . could . . . not get me . . ."

"C'mon Weber, are you that out of shape you fat bastard? Just take some time to breathe and then tell us the story so that we can hear the whole thing at once."

So Jeff and I waited there for a couple minutes, our eyes fixed upon Damian's mouth, waiting to hear how he managed to make 'the nearly impossible escape.' Finally, after regaining all form of consciousness and getting the color back into his face, he spoke his story.

"As I was saying, construction boy thought he had me. I had that piece of work of a bike and he had a car and the blue-collared lug head still couldn't get me. He was an inch behind me the whole time and I just kept pedaling as hard as possible. Yes sir because I didn't want to get caught this time. There was no way in hell that I was going to be the first one to get caught because I know the slack that I would have to take from you guys, always criticizing others, so I must admit, it made me work harder to achieve as you guys might s-"

Jeff spoke up. "Would you tell us the important stuff Rat Teeth?! Jus Ki!"

'Jus Ki' was supposed to mean 'Just Kidding', but Jeff and I said the words so fast that it came out as 'Jus Ki'. Nobody could really understand us when we said the words, which we said too often, but we didn't care. It was only important that we understood each other.

"O.K. . . . man . . . I simply pedaled my bike off the trail and into the ditch on that white trash guy's property over there. He's not gonna drive his car in the ditch so I must proudly say that I escaped the wrath of big construction boy."

While I laughed due to the aftershock of his escape, Jeff congratulated Damian.

"I'm impressed Rat Teeth. You must admit though, you were lucky he didn't get out and chase you. No offense, but you aren't the fastest guy in the world."

"Not as fast as you, right Jeff?" His tone was sarcastic and his voice was whiny, and I was once again annoyed by it. But I continued to ponder and reminisce on the success of our near faltering mission. Our mission was to harass the construction workers, and our mission was now complete.

Two of our friends had not come with us for the night. One of them was T.J. McBride and the other was John Suozzi. They were part of our five men E.B. gang, but T.J. had to work and John was with his girlfriend. All three of us agreed to chastise them for missing out. It made the bond between us three that much stronger for what we had accomplished together.

As we all talked, in the back of my mind I was still wallowing in my deep thoughts, the thoughts that were significant to me and nobody else. I thought about the bond between friends and how strong that bond truly is.

"Dude, let's go back to your house and play some SNK. We should get out of here just in case the cops come."

SNK was a baseball game my friends and I played on Nintendo. It was the best Nintendo game that we've ever known and we had a lot of good times with it, all the competitive seasons we'd played. Jeff loved the game. He loved to trash-talk in it when he would hit a homerun or win a game, so he naturally always brought up the idea to play.

So we jumped on our bikes, all except for Damian that is. He decided that walking would be the quickest and easiest way to get to my house, and I can't say that I disagreed. We then began our two-minute journey to my Nintendo.

On the way home, I remember looking into the sky and breathing clean, crisp air. Just looking at those stars made me realize how good the earth and God himself had been to me. Nothing could ruin the feeling I had then. The feeling that everything in the world was good and that nothing and nobody was out to hurt you. No fate, nor criminal, nor death was there to overtake you. And it was that moment which seemed to last forever, holding a permanent place in my memory until I reach that everlasting feeling in heaven.

Chapter Three

"Pass me a stogy." T.J. wasn't about to miss another good time. We had already told him about our successful mission two months ago, when the Kistner Concrete boys had chased us.

"Hey McBride . . ." Jeff waited for a reply, but T.J. was too busy lighting his cigar to pay attention to any disruption. "Hey McBride, how come you don't just put a couple stogies in your snout. This way you could smoke, talk, and play cards at the same time. Jus Ki, Jus Ki."

McBride is T.J.'s last name. We always made jokes about his nose because it pointed almost vertically to the sky; like it was the sensitive nose of a Labrador Retriever and it didn't want to miss the scent of alcohol. We sometimes even called him McSnout. He's 75% Irish and acted like one at times. He couldn't really handle his alcohol though. He would drink a couple and then act like he was completely sloshed. He would stumble all over the place and start slurring his words and stuff like that. We always thought he was joking. We had always planned to give him non-alcoholic beer and see if he still acted drunk, but the opportunity hadn't yet presented itself.

T.J. took a puff of his cigar and gently set it down on the ashtray, as he waited for a chance for the rest of us to stop laughing so that he could come back with something. Finally when it became quiet enough, he came back with a retort.

"I don't put the cigars in my nose because I'm scared that if

I sneeze, one cigar will pop out and give you a spot on the other cheek Nichols. Jus Ki, Jus Ki."

Nichols is Jeff's last name and we many times called him Spot because of a red birthmark on his left cheek. We had something to pick on everybody with. I had a crooked nose, which I broke in a ninth grade baseball practice. Our other gang member John Suozzi had a continuous, bushy eyebrow. It stretched from his left temple to his right. It thinned out a little in the middle, so it was hard to tell it was continuous from far away. But close up, one can see it's attached across his forehead through and through.

I laughed at McSnout's comeback until I noticed the below par hand of cards I had been dealt. Suozzi noticed my disappointment, so he had to say something.

"Looking a wee bit grim today there, Crook."

I looked up at him and mumbled out an evil chuckle. "Funny how I got this hand when you're the dealer you guinea, monobrow piece of shit!" I emphasized the last word to express my anger over the cards I received.

Then Jeff spoke out in the deep, mocking voice of his. "Now Crookedy Crook. I understand you're angry over the distorted shape of your nose, but there's no need to express this by taking it out on poor Suozz over there. Jus Ki, Jus Ki."

"O.K. Nichols, I'm gonna rip the spot off your cheek if you keep talking trash to me. Jus Ki, Jus Ki." I said my comment back the same way he spoke to me. We all had a specific kind of voice that we used when we were criticizing or threatening someone. It kind of made a mockery of them. It was kind of deep and actually a little bit like we were speaking as a mentally disabled person would. Not that we were mocking the mentally disabled, it just happened to be the voice that we used.

"O.K. fellas, let's ease it down a bit now. You're all here to lose in cards, not to harass each other."

"So McSnout, why don't you get down on your knees and

fulfill the reason you're here." I spoke kind of angrily as Suozzi was quietly laughing to himself.

"Wh-hat the hell are you talking about?"

"You look a little confused, McSnout . . . what I'm talking about is that you say we're here to lose to you in cards. Well, the only reason why we brought you here is because Jeff said that he wanted you to get down on your knees for him, so go and fulfill your duties."

Suozzi almost gagged on his freshly lit cigar after I made the comment. He broke out in laughter and Jeff laughed too, even though the joke involved him. McBride just kind of sat there drinking his 40-ounce of Old Milwaukee. I could only think to myself of how people will do anything to get drunk, even drink that piss water.

"I bet a dime on this hand." McBride was quick to change the subject and he figured that betting money was a good way to do that. So I just came back with another comment.

"You're a damn big spender McBride . . . why not just bet that roll of pennies you you have securely held in your hand."

Suozzi laughed even harder. I didn't think it was that funny myself, but I guess the fact that he was somewhat inebriated had a little to do with it. Whenever I'm drunk, I get the same way. I just laugh at anything.

"I'm out . . . I'm not gonna take the chance of losing a dime . . ." A slight pause followed Jeff's comment. We all stared at him, expecting him to say one of his just kidding's, but he never did. He was completely serious when he made the remark. So we all broke out in hysterics. Our laughs were resounding throughout the house, and it's quite a surprise that my mother didn't wake up. It was a pleasant surprise because she would not have been too pleased with a cellar full of alcohol and cigars.

McBride squeezed out a reply, but it took him a little while to get it out in between us hyenas. "You . . . scared little . . . bastard . . . ha, ha . . ." He gasped for a breath of air and then went on. "I was ridiculed for putting down a dime . . . ha, ha . . . and now you're scared to even do that, ha, ha, ha!"

"I agree with you McBride . . . ha, ha . . . but hey, maybe Nichols is saving up to buy a prostitute—his mother, ha!"

Jeff sat there for a while fuming with anger and trying to squeeze in a comeback, but he was unable to with the myriad of joking going on. But everybody heard him when he finally screamed out, "If I was looking for a prostitute, Crook, I'd just go to your girlfriend. The difference is, she'd give it to me for free. Jus Ki." Everybody else continued on with their drunken laughter, but I was far from finding the comment hysterical. I was more in hysteria, trying to pretend like I didn't care what he said, when I really did. My only comeback was minimal, because he was actually right about my girlfriend.

"Kiss my ass Nichols, that's all I gots to say. Jus Ki."

"Whoa, it's a good thing I showed up after all the dramatic escalation. I missed out on the foreplay but came just in time to see the fight." Hearing a voice from the stairway, everybody turned around to see Damian standing there, taking off his Salvation Army leather jacket.

"No, there's no fight. At least it wouldn't have been much of one, because I would've put Nichols down."

"O.K. Crook. You having trouble beating that little dick of yours, how are you gonna beat me?"

"You ever try and beat my dick. It's not easy to beat off something twice the length of your scrawny arms. Sometimes I have to use my feet to cop an orgasm."

"Oh yeah, I bet you-"

"Shut up McSnout, go to your duties of fulfilling Nichols' needs."

"Easy guys, I don't want to have to break up a fight again."

"Rat Teeth, how can you break up a fight when you can't even break that whiny ass voice of yours." McBride didn't have a chance to come back on my comment so he must've taken his frustrations out on Damian. If Damian had walked in when Jeff had ripped on my girlfriend, then I would have made Damian the center of ridicule, too. We all did this. Damian was like our gang's scapegoat.

"Oh fine, I just come in to try and bring the peace between you guys and somehow I'm the one to get harassed."

"Would you shut up Rat Teeth? Nobody wants to listen to your whiny voice." Jeff decided to join in on the ambush. Damian sat down with a helpless look, realizing his defeat against the onslaught of the E.B. boys.

"Gimme a beer. If you guys are gonna tear me apart, then at least let me be intoxicated."

"Great Rat Teeth, just take away your sorrows with a malt. Any chance of alcoholism in the family?" McBride had a point to his statement, but I must say that it was less cordial than Damian liked to hear.

"Oh, you're the one to talk T.J. You get drunk and caught, yet you drink some more because you feel bad about getting caught."

"That is true McSnout . . . after your parents caught you, ya just kept drinking and stealing liquor from that little bar of theirs."

"O.K. Suozzi, I see your point in that, but the funny thing is that when I steal liquor for you . . . you never seem to make that point then."

"Why should I? I have to use you for something. You getting caught won't get me in trouble."

Suozzi wasn't serious though. He was the type of kid who would stand by you if you got in trouble. I know that for a fact because once my mother caught me drinking downstairs with my friends, and when she asked where it came from; Suozzi was the first and only person to answer. He told her he brought some from home, which was a determinate lie. But since it was my mother and my house, he stuck up for me and took all the blame. Suozzi and I have had our disagreements in the past, but I respect him wholly for standing by his friends when it counts.

The game continued and so did our perpetual drinking. As

always happens with alcohol, people feel invincible and become careless. Well, we all became careless with our trash talking and began to say things that probably would've bothered us in most cases. But being in the condition we were, nobody took offense.

"Hey Crook, is it your girlfriend's turn to give a hummer to her black ex-boyfriend or to me?"

"Well Monobrow, you know what they say about Italians. They're the closest thing to a black man besides a black man himself, and you're Italian so that would explain her interest in you."

"They say that about Sicilians and you're Sicilian so that's why she's with you."

"Hey, did you say Unibrow was black or that your girlfriend went black and will never go back?" McBride was probably returning the knock that I gave him earlier and I must admit that he chose the right time, because then everybody joined in on the fun.

"She's got big tits, but big teeth too. I guess it's true about the saying, big damn teeth, big damn tits."

"Kiss my ass Spot, don't bring Rat Teeth's mother into this . . ." I had to bring the gang scapegoat into the quarrel in order to take the attention off of me. A couple "No, no, no's" came from Jeff and a lot of finger pointing went to Damian and as he always did when he got trashed on, he would come back with a whiny voice of, "How did I get into this?" And we all laughed and went on with our trash talking and card playing. But I had the last laugh.

"Ace and a two, I bet the whole pot . . . which I believe is now ten dollars in change." And the laughing stopped for a moment as I watched Suozzi turn over a ten, which gave me ten dollars in change to add to my account.

But the deadly silence didn't last long, because I'm afraid with intoxication, money and competition are of no consequence. In fact, once I scraped the money up into my hands, T.J. began laughing so hard; it sent our whole clan into mass confusion. I smiled at my oversized 1977 penny, which I used for good luck during poker.

I could barely make out the skinny face of Abe Lincoln, which was made all the more difficult by being under the influence of alcohol. But it gave me luck, so I just smiled at it and then looked up at Jeff. I realized then that Jeff looked somewhat like Abe Lincoln. Not his facial features, but the fact that he was somewhat scrawny like him. When I brought this up to him, there was another outpouring of criticisms from the crew, but this time all against Jeff. And so our game went on, and so we smoked and drank and basically had a merry ol' time.

Chapter Four

"C'mon Doug, I need the freakin' bathroom." My mom used that 'C'mon' word a lot. She emphasized the word and even changed her voice when she said it to add some dramatic affect, which became a faulty attempt to make it sound like she was really pissed off. The effect it had on people was of little value, though . . . because I just gave her a simple reply of, "I'm not quite done yet." The reply was always followed by a stamping of feet into the kitchen and the simultaneous muttering of words which could only be understood by the few religious leaders who knew how to speak in tongues.

I scratched the last bit of shaving cream off the surface of my chin, leaving a tiny, bloody trail, which accidentally looked like a cleft. "Shit, I barely have to shave and I cut myself every time I do."

I opened the door of the bathroom to make my exit, only to face a very impatient mother who planned to stay home anyway, but always needed something to complain about.

"Where are you going anyway?"

"This girl I know is having what's supposed to be a huge party. McBride and Jeff and Damian and Matt and John Suozzi are all supposed to be there, so I think I should be able to find someone to hang out with."

She closed the door behind her and kept speaking, even

through the trickle, trickle of her urination—which made it very difficult to understand her.

"Say it again mom, I can barely hear you . . ."

"What Doug?!"

"I said say it again so I can hear you!" I was screaming out and enunciating every word that I spoke.

"Are the parents gonna be there?"

"Doubtful, but if they were, what kind of party would that be?"

I then left her to explain some nonsense to herself, even though she thought she was talking to me. I went into my room to slide on my perfectly fitted 30-32 Arizona blue jeans and then flexed in the mirror, saying, "What an amazing piece of work God has made." It sounds a bit overconfident, but every man has a liking for himself . . . a somewhat cocky attitude. And even though they might not express it openly, they're feeling it inside.

"I'm outtie, mom . . ."

"O.K. hon, have fun and I love you."

"Love you too mom." It's funny how when mothers say that they love you; they won't say another word to you until you say it back to them. It's almost as if they only say it to you so that they can feel loved. But mothers are a great part of life nonetheless, and without their caring nature, every human being would be a lost dog.

After driving for about fifteen minutes while listening to high-bass rap music, I pulled into the driveway of the party. It looked quite small at first glance, but with all my close friends there, it had a lot of promise for a drunken bonding event.

"Here's a beer Doug." McBride had been able to hold his liquor much better lately, and he was always the first one to offer a beer. Even though he rarely paid for it, I was still impressed with his courtesy.

"Good to see everybody in such high spirits this evening."

"What do you mean?"

"You all look bored, that's what I mean. Ahhhhh, I know the problem."

"Lack of alcohol . . ."

"Lack of alcohol . . ."

"Lack of alcohol . . ."

T.J., Jeff, and I spoke nearly simultaneously. It was no wonder, though. We thought the same, especially when it came to alcohol.

"Hey, where's the beer? I need one more. I like to be double fisted."

"You mean like when you masturbate Crook? Jus Ki." Nichols was quite the little smart-ass. He rarely came back with a sly comment, but when he did, it was always a good one that would make everybody laugh and ultimately causing the victim of his jokes to feel like the biggest idiot.

I chuckled myself and then made my way toward the garage, where someone had directed me to the nearest keg. I filled both my hands with a full cup, only to turn around and have somebody ask me to play beer games with them. Not wanting to be a coward, I accepted the challenge. After awhile, I kind of lost track of the outer world. I guess that's what people call a black out, but that was my first time ever experiencing one, so I never understood before the horrible feeling that they were referring to—that helpless feeling when you wake up the next morning and don't really know what occurred the night before. I was lucky to have my friends around though, so they could guide me to safety.

"Let's go to Mickey D's and grab something to eat."

"Great idea, Nichols . . . let's go to the place where McSnouter works." My words came out more slurred than I would have liked and it was probably difficult for people to understand what I was trying to say, especially since drunken people mumble on about nonsense and others laugh at them because they're acting so ridiculous. But what I recall trying to explain, was actually that I was making a sad attempt at trash talking T.J.'s job.

Jeff was the only completely sober one, so he was the chauffeur to McDonalds. On our way there, I remember riding in the old, rusty piece. It was a red truck of the 80's, except it was no longer the 80's and the truck acted as such. The wheel made a slight, screeching sound with every turn. The sound was magnified by a hole that rusted through the right corner of the truck, so that every passenger felt the wind of the engine, whether or not the heat was on. The interior wasn't even up to par, with the radio hanging out of its deck and the rearview mirror on the dashboard rather than suction cupped onto the window. I remember commenting on the truck in my unstable condition.

"You better hope you don't ever get in an accident with this piece . . . you'll have no chance for survival."

"You wouldn't have any chance for survival . . . but when you're built like me, you have no worries. Jus Ki, Jus Ki."

T.J. attempted to throw in the last word as the inebriated always do. "Yeah right Jeff, you're a freakin' twig. Jus Ki."

"O.K. McSnout. You're hanging over your belt buckle with fat so I don't think you're one to comment." He spoke like he was upset, which he sometimes did to make a conversation more dramatic. But it was difficult to make Jeff upset. He rarely fought, but never tried to make peace between people either. He just sat back and watched the soap opera of other people; all the while living out his own in his own way. McBride didn't answer to his reply, probably because he was too drunk to care.

"Jeff, what are you doing?!" Two headlights from an 18-wheeler truck began barreling down on us. Jeff, who was looking toward T.J. and barely paying attention to his driving, fiercely grabbed the wheel with two hands rather than his thumb that he had been using, then quickly maneuvered his truck back into the correct lane. The 18-wheeler sped past with a powerful vengeance and an angry beep of its horn.

"Whoo-hoo, that was wild!" T.J. exclaimed in his drunken state, unable to understand that his body could have been a human s'mores between the jaws of metal and steel rather than a skeletal structure with inner organs and an exterior of skin. I was terrified, and though drunk, I was capable of understanding the mortality of a human being.

Jeff looked more embarrassed than anything. His face held a tone of red while his lips transformed from pink to a ghostly white.

"You're the sober one?" I had to ask, though I knew he only had two beers over a two to three hour period. "Maybe T.J. should drive?" My voice trembled slightly and Jeff chuckled at my comment, thinking I was joking; but I was wholly serious.

"Lucky for you Crook, we're here. My plan didn't work out. Jus Ki, Jus Ki."

His truck, actually an engine with a rusty exterior, pulled into McDonald's and gently idled its way into a parking place. I stumbled out the door with my blurred vision and somehow made my way into the restaurant and ordered some burgers. I reached into my pocket for some loose change, only to realize that my last ounce of money had been spent on beer.

"Anybawdy have sim spare change for a poor drunken man?"

Jeff was somewhat of a tightwad, but he would lend another money if beer was the root cause of their need for welfare. "I have some scroungy. I know you won't pay me back so I'll just have to steal it from you sometime. Jus Ki."

"You talk too clearly for me Spot. I can't understand sober people." I was beginning to talk more clearly all of a sudden. It was more from being drunk so long rather than the fact that I was sobering up. Meanwhile, T.J. was over in the corner, unable to recognize anything that was going on around him.

"You gonna have me up to college this year?"

"Of course I will Spotter . . . just as long as you don't get me in trouble. We can't pull any of that East Bethany gang shit up there. The cops don't know us quite as well."

"No, I won't. I just want to come up and have a good time. Drink a little . . . drink a little more . . . then go back to your dorm and pass out . . . Jus Ki!"

I looked at him as he spoke and felt a chill cascade itself

upon my neck, kind of like a ghost had just touched me, telling
me to 'wake up and smell the coffee.' Why it was telling me that,
I don't know. Probably because I was drunk so it was telling me
to be responsible. But I just couldn't get over the way I felt then—
the presence of something there from the future warning me, or
maybe even guiding me, to some thought or idea. But I ignored
the strange feeling, throwing it off and using my intoxication as
an excuse. I then swung my head to face T.J., almost in slow
motion. But all I saw was T.J. wallowing in his own drool . . . the
sticky, white mess coming off the recently sanitized tables, only
to be sucked back up into his slobbering jaws every time he
breathed in. I turned back to Jeff, and then down to my freshly
grilled cheeseburger. I grabbed it between my two hands and
attempted to inhale it, just in case it wasn't there tomorrow. I
wanted to enjoy everything that life had to offer, while I could
and while life would give it. I wouldn't want to go to my afterlife
without experiencing the best of what earth had. I'd be embarrassed to be sitting around a table after I die . . . a table with all
the other after-lifers. And they'd be talking about winning the
high school basketball championship, or doing donuts with some
car in a field, and all the other great fun things in life, no matter
how dangerous. They'd be talking about all these experiences
with so much enthusiasm. Yet there I would be. They'd ask me,
"What's your exciting experience in life?" And I'd say, "My
dreams."

It's good to have dreams. I'm just afraid that I won't live long
enough to fulfill them. So I take something when I have the chance
for it and I hold onto it, fighting for it until the last chance of
winning it is gone. I take that risk and many times get hurt in the
process. But I still take that chance and when time heals my
hurt, I can always look back and be proud that I have never quit
on a dream. I'm just scared that I will never be able to fulfill all of
my dreams . . . scared to die before I get the chance.

Chapter Five

"Doug, hurry up! You're late for everything!" I was finally off to college on a pleasantly incandescent day. I was going to SUNY Brockport to begin my studies, with no clarity as to the new realm of study I was entering into. But people say to depart from home to experience college and then determine what subjects are of interest to you. And hey, with all the freedom away from home and the partying that goes on at colleges, I wasn't about to disagree with the logic.

"Doug, I'm gonna leave without ya if you don't get your ass out here!" Moms always act like they're in a hurry to get you out of the house, but once you're actually about to leave, they miss you like crazy. Women are basically stubborn though, so I guess it's the same with a mother.

They give you all the love you need as a child, but as you grow older, they act like they can't wait to get rid of you. And they act this way up until the second you're about to leave, which is when they say, "You're not gonna leave without a hug and a kiss, are ya?" So you turn around for the hug and kiss and their eyes are watering with tears, and their lip starts to curl up trying to hold back the tears. It's then that you realize how much your mother misses you. You realize then that the only reason why mothers pretend they want you out of the house is so that it isn't so traumatic on themselves—the fact that they're losing one of their children to the real world. The fact that a part of them will no longer be with them every minute of the day, pestering them to find a lost toy, or for five dollars to go to the movies, or even to give some advice on a problem. It's such a peculiarity—the way in which mothers deal with the 'Empty Nest Syndrome'.

I grabbed my last suitcase off the floor. It was a brand new suitcase that I had gathered from my birthday, but already had pet hair stuck to the fabric. I began my journey to the car, which was also packed with my sister's belongings because we were both attending the same college.

But before I did, I made one last turn around to look at the house, and the sheltered, predictable life that I was leaving behind. Things were changing so much in my life. I was growing up and maturing. My friends seemed so distant from me now. T.J. had found a girlfriend named Wendy and was spending most of his time with the cute, little blonde. Damian found a new bunch of friends from the small city of Batavia, which was very close to East Bethany. John Suozzi and I never could seem to get along, and had split apart over time.

We would always fight over dumb things, too. Once we almost had a fistfight over whether or not the Mafia was a very intelligent criminal group. I stated that they weren't intelligent, they were just very prosperous and powerful. He tried to explain something about how they started, that they hadn't been that way when the group had first started, that they started off as a very sneaky and intelligent group. But I was quite stubborn in my younger years and I wouldn't give people a chance to explain their own point of view. When I wouldn't let him explain his beliefs, it made him quite angry. So he jumped up and walked out onto the street, screaming at me to come out and challenge him. I told him to relax and my friends did too, so he sat down and told me not to say another word. I made one last comment about how, "you don't say a word and I won't say a word," and the escalation simmered down at that point. So we never actually had a brawl, but it was petty things like that which made us come close to brawling many times, and which ultimately led to our separation.

As for Jeff, he and I just didn't see each other as much anymore. Out of all my close friends, I probably maintained the closest attachment to him. But even we seemed to unintentionally detach ourselves from each other. We would go to a recreation park and play tennis once in awhile, or play baseball at our high school field. Sometimes I would go over and play basketball with him, but I began to talk to his older brother more than him. It's bound to happen after high school. Everybody goes their own way, and those that are still in high school or that stay home the year after they graduate seem to find new friends or acquaintances to compensate for the ones they've lost.

I realized then that the only thing I was truly leaving behind was my dog Harley. I loved the dog with all my heart. We named him Harley after the motorcycle because he was so fast when he was younger. He was only up to my knees when standing up and had blonde hair, but a white breast. He was part terrier, and the rest of him was full-bred mutt.

I heard from my eleventh grade social studies teacher once, that an American was just like a mutt. They had a combination of all the best qualities of every nationality, or from a dog's perspective, it would be a combination of all the best canines. Every dog has their own specific talents, which God had made particularly for their breed. When those talents are mixed together, as with a mutt, they get every talent or specialty that every breed has to offer.

That is the way Harley was and still is in his old age. He's nine years old now and still just as rambunctious as when he was in his youth. I swear though, he must have the canine equivalent of a human Irishman—a little crazy and very stupid, because the dog is the bravest bastard that I know. He will fight with anything and everything and never give up until it's either broken up or until the death.

I still remember a time when he was probably about five

years old. It was a dark night and everything was very quiet in our little town. In other words, it was the perfect night for the most successful night prowlers, also known as wild animals, to gain their prestige and adoration by catching the nightly snack. I remember my dog just roaming around our yard, and then all of a sudden, I heard successive barking. My dog has a certain bark where he warns of danger, and it was that bark. Then I heard growling, so my mother and I went outside to see what was happening.

To our surprise, my dog was fighting with three wild dogs. I remember seeing six wild eyes of fiery rage surrounding my little Harley and trying to attack him from all sides. But my dog didn't give up and was putting up an impressive fight. The only determinant to the fight was my mother running out with a wiffle ball bat in one hand and a stick in the other, screaming at the other dogs to "get away from our Harley!" The wild dogs gazed at her for a moment and then skiddadled off into the fields, probably to find an easier target for a nightly snack.

It was this brave and courageous dog that I would miss the most going to college. Everybody has something in life that's special to them, and my fat, little Harley is most special to me. He's the one who has experienced nearly everything in my life with me, and the one who has remained by my side through it all. I love something I can trust. I despise the whole idea of betrayal, and my dog is one of only a few that I can trust to remain loyal and not betray me.

My mother's voice was echoing in my ears. I could hear her scream and complain, sounding like the drum from the Energizer bunny, a repetitive pummeling of bass pounding in my ear. I tightened the grip onto my suitcase and made a sharp turn toward the car. I didn't want to turn around and torture myself over what I was leaving behind any longer. I found myself in a fast-paced walk toward the car, threw my fully packed suitcase into the trunk, and then sat in the car and slammed the door behind me, only to feel even more depressed than I had the whole summer.

I didn't enjoy my summer much before college. The only pleasurable experience was a trip to Virginia Beach that I had made with the family. But before that, I had found out that the girl I had been dating was cheating on me with her ex-boyfriend. Even after going through hell with that whole situation, I tried to stay with her because I don't like to quit on anything. I can't deny it's also because I had been trying to get her for six months, and I really didn't see the purpose of putting all that time to waste. I tried to meet girls in Virginia Beach, but didn't succeed. Then when I came home, I was hired for a job at a theme park. I hated the job because I was in food service and I always worked in a stand by myself, sitting there for hours on end in a cramped up booth doing nothing but twiddle my thumbs, wonder what my fantasies for the upcoming night would be about, and wait to serve customers who rarely came. And then, the girl I had been dating decided that there was really nothing to our relationship anymore. We had been through too much and the only choice we had was to end our already dying relationship. I was depressed and glad at the same time. Too many problems came out of the time I spent with her; she was not trustworthy whatsoever. I talked about the importance of loyalty to me. Well, she was far from loyal which brought about feelings of discontent between us. I was glad because a gruesome era in my life had ended, leaving me with nothing at home except a fight for integrity—and my loyal dog, of course.

I thought of this all the way up to college. I didn't know what I wanted out of life. I felt like a leaf floating in the wind, with a gleam of fire in my eyes, yet not knowing what direction to expend my energy towards. You hear songs on the radio and they make you think of a moment in your past, whether good or bad. But there are no songs that make you think about a moment in the future. While I was in the car watching scenery pass by me, I tried to think about what I wanted in my future, even though all the songs on the radio kept giving me flashbacks of my past summer. So I was glad when my mother's '94 Dodge Intrepid pulled up to the McLean freshman dorm. It gave me something new to think about. The college scene was exasperating and soothing at the same time. The thought of having to do everything by myself built up an empire of stress, but the realization of my freedom and the many new people and experiences that I would meet gave me a sense of consolation. I was on my own in a dreadful, do-or-die world. I was up for the challenge and wasn't about to let anything stop me from enjoying my first year of liberty.

My mother helped me with my bags and refused a chance for help by some of the college janitorial workers. She said that, "they have enough to do without our petty bags being a nuisance." I followed with no complaints; I didn't have much to carry anyway.

I walked into my room and was met by my high school friend Matt, and found relief in the comfortable surroundings that I had advanced into. The room was symmetrical. A line could have been drawn down the middle of it if I had wanted to keep everything separated from my roommate. Each bed was placed crosswise from each other with one desk on each end, and two dressers blocking the sight of a dying tree outside.

"This room is too congruent or something. It's too neat."

Matt sighed an agreeable sigh before replying. "You're right, but I'm too lazy to change it."

"Your laziness is noted and believe me, you are not alone." We chuckled a little with the agreed upon laziness between us. We weren't out to impress people. It gave us a place to sleep and hide away, and that was our only concern.

I began to unpack while my mother was inspecting the dorm. She made comments on some of the girls that went by, whether or not they were up to my standards. I couldn't hold back my smile while she was talking; it made me realize all the opportunities I had. My past could be left in my past. The high school sweetheart who had caused me nothing but trouble could hopefully be forgotten and my new life of success could start. After an hour of visiting, my mother and sister decided to leave so that my sister could move into her dorm. The door shut behind them, crashing with a vengeance and leaving me to ponder my excitement. I was here with my newfound freedom. So I kissed my hand and sent it up to God.

"What exactly are you doing?" Matt's voice sounded as if I just had a nervous breakdown.

There was only one thing I could say. "I am thanking the one who has given me a life."

He laughed and nodded his head, then added a comment of his own. "I'll drink to that!"

"Believe me . . ." A deviant grin widening on my face. "I will continue to drink to that throughout this year." I flattened onto my bed, falling as if I had reached the highest point of exhaustion, yet smiling and feeling energy escalating through my veins. A happy energy. No anger and no bitterness. Just crazy energy.

Chapter Six

I hadn't been home yet during the college year. Brockport was only a half-hour from East Bethany, so I'm not sure of the reasoning. Probably because the weekends were too enjoyable, going out with friends and drinking at the bars, basically acting like an idiot. I enjoyed that stuff. That's my idea of a good time. But anyway, I had to go home for the weekend, the main reason being that my clothes had gotten dirty and I didn't feel like spending two dollars to wash them.

I was going home with a hangover. The night before, I had gone to a bar called Northbound for Happy Hour. They have a Happy Hour every Friday night. One of the fraternities pay for it, but then each person has to pay five dollars to get in for three hours worth of all the drinking they want. Some of the pretty girls get in for free, though. Especially if they smile real nice and probably even promise a couple favors to the bouncers for the upcoming night. Nonetheless, it's still a good deal. The only downfall is that they serve the cheapest beer, Old Milwaukee. It tastes horrible, but it gets you drunk and at college, that's the main purpose of going out.

But I was going home for a relaxing weekend. It was time to ease my spirits so that I wouldn't be too hyper to do anything when I got to East Bethany. My sister and I went home about three o'clock. We got a ride with Jeff's mother. She worked at the college and was normally the one to take us home, and then one of my parents would bring us back on a Sunday night. She usually brought us home on a Friday because she didn't work on the weekends, but it just so happened that she fell behind in her work that particular week, and she had a lot of catching up to do, so she decided to work on her day off. It seems odd how some things work out so perfectly. I mean, it's unfortunate for her that she had to come in on her day off, but at least it gave my sister and I a chance to go to Happy Hour. "Something good always comes out of bad" is my motto, and one that certainly came true in this circumstance.

Jeff's mother is Kathy. She was quite pretty for a mother actually. I guess all those jokes we made about Jeff's mother had some truth to them. After all, my friend Damian once told me that there's a little truth in everything one says. Well, I don't believe in that, but it definitely had some validity in her case. She looked healthy for her age. I don't know exactly how old she was, but any mother with older teenagers is usually above thirty. She was in great shape, with a youthful face, and hair that was curly brown, but so dark it could be classified as black. She probably looked so good because she always went jogging and played tennis with the family. Any sport is bound to keep someone healthy.

We didn't talk much on the way home. Everybody was recuperating from the hard work during the week, and for my sister and I, from our previous rough night. I was rejuvenated when I found out after pulling in the driveway, that Jeff was home. It made me kind of happy because I hadn't seen any of my friends in so long. I opened the clunky door of the rusted van, and jumped out to see what Jeff was up to. To my surprise, he was helping his father put up an electrical fence for their dog. "Damn it Jeff, hold it steady." Jeff's father is one of the most unique people I ever met. His physical features consisted of a man about five foot ten, hair that was curly yet always fashionably combed.

He was fairly built and very healthy, just like his wife. But then again, he worked as a physical education teacher, explaining his interest in physical fitness for the whole family. They were all in great shape. They always did things together as a family, like going to parks and playing sports, or even just having a little get together to hang out, drink, and talk with each other. The Nichols had three sons. One was Jeff, the oldest was Steve, and the youngest was Todd. Their dad spent time with them whenever he could. He thought of sports as vital to a kid's growing up, and he would almost beg the kids to come outside and practice with him. A great father, as well as teacher for his school. There are countless times that he was in the paper for doing something for the community, or helping youths with a difficult time in their lives. He's just an all around good man. Nothing less and much more. I played Babe Ruth baseball for him from age thirteen to seventeen. One distinct characteristic I remember about his coaching style was his relaxed tone of voice. He couldn't sound angry if he wanted to. I remember him telling one of the players to "hustle after the ball." He tried to scream it out, but it ended up as more of a motivational talk rather than an angry scream. I personally think that he has the best type of coaching style. I bring it up because it was this relaxed voice that he was using with Jeff when they were putting up the fence. "Jeff, I said to hold it still and level . . . If . . . if you don't hold it still and level, then I'll get shocked."

"Better you than me. Jus Ki, Jus Ki," Jeff replied. The prominent father-son attitude was showing in full effect.

I had to interrupt the momentous father-son bonding experience with a, "Listen to the 'ol man Jeff, he's wise in his old age. Jus Ki, Jus Ki." This was followed with a sarcastic grin by Jeff's father, Gary, and a high burst of laughter from Jeff.

"Hey Doug," he said, dropping his work and sending a small voltage of electricity through his father.

"Damn it Jeff. You want to get shocked?" This was followed by another high-pitched outburst of laughter from Jeff, and then a mutual agreement between the two to go inside and take a break so that they could talk with my sister and I.

"So how's the brother-sister combination doing at college?"

Gary asked in his relaxed voice that would normally put someone to sleep, but made you stay awake by keeping you interested
in what he was talking about.

"Is going anywhere with Doug a pleasurable experience?,"
my sister replied.

Jeff followed with another high-pitched outburst of laughter
and then a, "No, no, no, no, no." He would always say those
'no's' quickly and mockingly. Whenever somebody was trash-
talking somebody else, he would always throw those mocking
'no's' in there just to add excitement to the criticism. So I interjected my own statement or two in order to stay away from the
'scapegoat syndrome.' That syndrome where you're the chosen
one for the day to be ridiculed. You have to escape the syndrome
early, because once you fall behind and everybody gets a chance
to crack a joke about you, ya minds well forget it, because you've
already caught the syndrome.

"Actually my sister loves me there, as I love her there." I
thought flattery would keep everybody away from the trash talking. "We actually hang out quite a bit together at the bars."

"Aren't you kiddies a wee bit young for the bars?" Gary said
this with a smile, letting us know that he was just kidding. He
then laughed one of his strange laughs. It sounded like Charles
Ingalls on the TV show, "Little House on the Prairie." It started
off with a sharp ha, and then no sound could be heard for a few
seconds. Until finally an asthmatic wheezing would come out,
which normally lasted for about ten seconds. This led to a normal laugh, the full-blown 'ha, ha's'. It was more of a smoker's
laugh, but Gary Nichols was far from a smoker. Like I said, he
was a physical education teacher and very involved in the health
of human beings, especially his children. The only thing he did
was drink, and even that was only at social occasions.

We all laughed at his joke, too. We realized that he understood our generation, as sad as it was. But we were a drinking
generation. There's no denying that. It's nothing to be proud of
nor is it anything to be ashamed of. Our generation knows how to

have fun, and drinking is one way in which we do that. It was nice and somewhat relieving to meet parents who understood that, and while they didn't encourage the act, they also didn't condemn it.

"Would you like to see our new dog fence? I'm sure Jeff would be happy to show you how it works." He once again put on a performance of his special laugh and then went on to say something more. "It's pretty much finished, except it isn't put in the place where we want it yet, so be careful where you walk." His laugh once again superseded what he said. Jeff picked on him this time, as the family many times did . . . always making a mockery out of each other to get a chuckle out of their audience.

"H . . . h-h-h-h-h-h-h-h-h-h-haaaaaaaahaaaahahahaha. Dad, you sound like you're ready to die when you laugh like that. I know you're an aging old man, but at least try and keep your laugh young . . . especially when that's all you have left."

"No, no, no, no, no Mr. Nichols," I followed up with in order to arouse the provocation. Gary just nodded his head in help-lessness.

"Make fun of me now while you're young. You don't have long before you reach my age, believe me. It goes by fast," he said.

Jeff quickly retorted, "Dad, we have a long way 'til we reach you. The only thing we might be close to is the beer gut you've been sporting with all the beer we've been drinking. Jus Ki. Jus Ki." We all had to laugh at that one, even Gary himself. He then told Jeff to get out and show me the fence, probably to escape the 'scapegoat syndrome'.

I followed Jeff out the screen door and into their backyard. We had shared many good times together in that yard. I kept walking and suddenly I noticed with my peripheral vision that Jeff had stopped. I felt like a dog on the prowl looking for something, but I didn't really know what I was looking for.

"What's up, Spot?" I lapsed into a zone with my eyes planted on Jeff's next movement.

"Here Crook, take this dog collar . . . I . . ." He looked confused about something so I grabbed the dog collar and continued in his footsteps. "I swear . . . I . . ."

"Ouch!" I threw the dog collar down after feeling voltage run through my fingertips and into my wrist, leaving my hand to twitch from the eerie ghost that tortured me. I noticed that Jeff was in hysterical laughter on the ground, this time almost sounding like his father without even trying. He was rolling around, getting grass stains on his one size too small T-shirt, and kicking out his legs seemingly to release some of his energy.

"You bastard . . . you . . . you . . ." I couldn't seem to release my words due to the shock that my friend had just played a genius prank on me. "You gave me the dog collar just so I would get shocked . . .", my mouth still opened in awe that I could be so gullible. Jeff darted for the door before I got a chance to get revenge, and began telling the story to his parents and my sister. By the time I realized what was happening, he had already finished. I opened the screen door to get back inside only to see everybody already pointing fingers at me, finding the accused guilty with no trial. I could only smile, realizing the inequity of my situation.

"You'll get yours Jeff . . . someday you'll receive the shock . . . and when you least expect it, too." I proceeded with a defiant stare to make my threat more believable, which brought out a bunch of 'oohs' and 'ahhs' from the gatherers. Jeff and I hadn't had enough fun yet, so we went back outside to bond somewhere over our electrifying friend.

I got shocked a couple more times and Jeff only once. But that was enough for him. After he tried it once, he decided that it was made for the dog for a good reason.

Jeff and I decided we had enough of our torture toy, so we walked back inside, emotionally and physically drained. "If we're still on the conversation of beer, I would like to add some input."

"What's that, Crook?"

"Well, I'd like to input some beer into my stomach to replenish myself, that's all."

"Is it to replenish yourself or to numb the feeling in your body so that you could go out and prove your manliness again?" My sister added in a joke of her own with a little smirk to provoke me. I smiled back. I knew how careless I was.

The front door slammed and the figure of Steve Nichols filled the doorway. Steve was older than Jeff by about two years and a genius in every way. He was a great athlete, too, although he didn't play any sports in college. But he participated in soccer and track in high school, and was one of the fastest people that I've ever seen. He stood about five foot ten like his father, with brown hair and preppy style clothing. He was a prototype yuppie. He wore expensive clothing, and had an intellectual, yet stud-type image. His interests lay in business, politics, and law. It suits him perfectly because he is the smoothest speaker that I have ever known. The kid is going to be an amazing politician someday. He's got a lot of charisma. He could talk his way out of a paper bag if he had to. I would start an intellectual conversation with him sometimes for the lone reason of trying to catch him off guard. I would try and make him stutter over his own words, and every time I would come up with a good point or idea, and feel that I caught him off guard, he always has and will come up with something to downplay my conclusion. He would then come up with his own point or idea, and make it sound so obvious, as if somebody should have thought of it before. But his ideas are so genius that nobody is capable of thinking of such things.

He and my sister used to date in high school. It was one of those high school loves, and believe me, they were deeply in love. But college changes a lot, as well as the meaning in a relationship. It's difficult to stay with one person when there are so many others out there to experiment with. As traumatic as it is on two people, many go through it once they hit college. They both realized the impossibility of trusting and being faithful to one another, so they chose to remain friends. Friends who fought all the time like a quarreling married couple. Sometimes I wonder if they'll get married. They seem so good together at times, yet so bad at others. I guess there's only one man who knows the future though, but he's not really a man. But for explanatory purposes, I'm referring to the man upstairs.

"Hello Nichols family, as well as those who have chosen to join our happy home." He turned his head to the side as he spoke, in that cocky way that he had. It was one of his trademarks to be cocky and he always expressed it with a turn of his head, or a laugh, or something that would make you want to grab his neck and explain to him that he walks on two feet just like everybody else. But honestly, that's one trait that I respect about him, is his ability to carry himself and maintain control at all times. He never allows anger to divert his attention. Or if he did, he would never let on. And he always maintained control when in a conversation with somebody. He would never shout or stand up so that he could get people's attention. He didn't need to. He always made sense and explained himself thoroughly and fluently, so people just naturally listened when he spoke.

My sister retaliated against his arrogant entrance with a killer's stare. I just tried to come back with a comment to bring down his ego. "Looking mighty frat-boyish with the preppy clothes that you're sportin'." He hated being called a frat-boy. He claims that "not all fraternities are the same, and just because one fraternity might use hazing as a means of initiation, not all of them do." And he insists that the fraternity he is in is a "suitable organization to supply the student body with its necessary accommodations", or something to that effect. The 'accommodations' that he is referring to, in my opinion, is alcohol. I can't see any other purpose for his fraternity. But then again, saying that is a statement for his fraternity rather than against it.

"Hey, when you look good, you may as well dress good. After all, my far superior intelligence isn't what gets the ladies to follow me home." My sister was outraged with jealousy at his comeback. She closed her lips together in a pout, and then walked up to him and repeatedly punched him in the arm, all the while he was saying with a smile on his face, "What did I say? Did I say something wrong?"

I had to chuckle at the scenario. He and my sister were always trying to say things to enrage one another.

Steve's younger brother Todd walked down the stairs from his room. He was eleven years old, but already taller than me. He was about five foot nine. He had fairly broad shoulders, which are sure to broaden up even more by the time he's grown up. He was a nice kid, but brutally honest in his opinion, like all eleven-year olds tend to be. "Doug and Kristie are here?" He asked this as if he was annoyed by our presence.

Gary interjected with a statement. "You must have heard Kristie and Steve fighting, ha? Ha-h-h-h-h-h-hhahahahahaha!"

"Dad, you must do something about that laugh." Todd had a tendency to criticize other people, but once you criticized him, he would get very defensive. He was an amazing athlete though, and that's the perfect attitude for an amazing athlete to have. I guess you could say it's kind of a competitive attitude. In a game, you want to attack the other team and will do nearly everything in your power to succeed at that. But if the other team succeeds against you, then you become angry. Well, it's the same way in a war of words. He did everything in his power to degrade the other person, but when he was the one being degraded, he would always get defensive and start throwing a tantrum.

"Grandma Nichols!" Steve screamed out in pure exhilaration. "Grandma Nichols, so glad you could come and join our fiesta."

Grandma Nichols was like a second grandmother to my sister and I. She owned some apartments about a mile from where we lived, so we would sometimes jump in the car and take a drive over there to see how things were going. Or if we felt bored or simply needed someone to talk to, we would go over there and see her. And she was always willing to take time out of her schedule to visit with us. There was one time she went on vacation to Cape Cod with the family, so she asked me to mow her acre lawn for her while she was gone, with the notion that she would pay me an impressive sum of money. Well, the lawnmower broke down so I couldn't quite finish the job. I figured maybe I should get ten dollars for the work that I did. Well, she ended up giving me forty dollars "just for the effort." I felt kind of guilty for taking it, but the temptation of greed was overwhelming.

She had gray hair and a very loving face, and a loving heart to go with it. You could tell she was probably quite busty as a young lady. She was a little bottom heavy, as grandmothers many times are, and she walked with a slight wobble that was barely noticeable. She always joked around with the kids, which would many times result in a punch to old granny's arm, or a criticism to her age. But she took everything as a big joke. She took everything in stride and was quite a relaxed old lady. I suppose that explains why her son Gary was so relaxed. It was passed down through genetics.

Her husband, Norm, hobbled in behind her. It's been said that Norm was a stud in his younger years, and I believe every story that I hear about him. I remember a time when I played poker with him, Steve, and some of Steve's friends. Grandpa Norm was the life of the party. He had some of the most hilarious sayings in poker. He would first ask you if you had any money, and without any idea why he was asking, you would say, "Well yeah, I have ten bucks." He was always quick to reply with a, "Well, C'mon then, let's play some poker." And then he would throw in a little element of dare and say, "Or are ya scared you're gonna lose all your money?" He would always sucker you into playing, but believe me, once you started playing with this guy, you wouldn't want to stop. The whole night, we were all laughing at his sayings that were so full of wisdom, and his challenges to place higher bets. He had some special words of wisdom for every play that happened in poker. I remember I lost one hand, and he said, "Well, you know what they say fellas . . . some days you just can't piss a drop." I remember the moment clearly. I was upset because I had just lost two dollars on the hand, but hearing him talk and joke around put me in good spirits.

Norm was about Steve's height. He still had some brown hair showing through the overbearing gray. He always walked kind of slow, not because he was relaxed; but because he had diabetes. And diabetes at his age made him very slow—and forgetful. I wondered sometimes if he had Alzheimer's disease, but the doctors insisted that it was caused by his diabetes. Norm fought on a plane in World War II. I believe it was a B-27 bomber, because he had a white hat with large blue lettering on it, which said B-27. He would tell stories sometimes and talk about how it was being caught in the action. He was a brave young fella, and still is even in his old age. Jeff was the closest to him out of the three children. They would always joke around back and forth about who could win in poker, or who was better at baseball at seventeen years old. When Jeff was the one to go out and mow his grandmother's lawn, Norman would always come out and help him start up the lawnmower because sometimes it wouldn't work. So Norm would be out there swearing and trying to explain what might be wrong, and Jeff would just smirk at him, realizing that his grandfather didn't have the first damn clue what was wrong with the lawnmower. Norm was a near perfect fit to the family puzzle, but the one thing he differed on with every member of the family was that he was a die hard Democrat. The rest of the family always quarreled with him on political ideas and laws. He insisted that the Democrats were truly out for the people, and even when Steve proved him wrong with another one of his brilliant explanations, Norman would still defend the honor of the Democrats.

In fact, the first topic of conversation that Steve brought up with his grandfather that day was that Bill Clinton was caught in another scandal. Die-hard Democrat Norman explained that it was a sick attempt by the Republicans to decrease his popularity with the American people. Now I admit that politics is filled with lying and scams to decrease popularity of the opposing politician, but I disagreed with Norman in this scenario, basically because I myself am not a fan of Bill Clinton.

The '94 Dodge Intrepid idled into the driveway. My mom had come to pick us up and bring us home. I really liked her car. It was glossy black with a cloth interior. The radio was mantled with a tape deck. In front was a built-in tape holder and two-cup holders, which could also be used as an armrest. It had power windows, power locks, and all the great essentials to a modern day car. I have an owner's attachment to my car, and definitely prefer the way it handles to my mother's. But sometimes, I would use her car for its polished appearance. It's quite invigorating when you're driving along the street and you stop at a red light, only to look over and see a beautiful brunette checking out your car. Then she looks up and sees you in there and displays the most seductive smile. You could take the opportunity, but the intelligent thing to do would be to drive off and forget about her, and realize that she only wanted you for the car. But such is the enjoyment of life. If people like you for something that you have and not for you, yourself— you let them get just close enough to what they want without quite getting it, and then you walk away. Or with a car, you drive away. This way they ponder over their loss and you end up with a feeling of pride, hoping that maybe you taught them something. Although often, people never learn and they continue to live their lives repeating past mistakes and failures.

My mom got out of the car, slammed the door shut, and walked to the house, hurrying as if she was distressed about something. But once she entered the house, she seemed to relax instantaneously. A smile broadened across her worried face, and she became extremely friendly and began talking about how she was happy to drive over and find herself at a party. My mom was always one for going out and enjoying herself. She liked to have get-togethers and is a great hostess when she does have them.

She was a dedicated mother. She had a job as a counselor working with veterans with disorders such as PTSD, so she was always there to talk with us if we needed her. Personally, I didn't like to talk about my problems too much, and I don't think my sister did either, but it was still nice knowing that somebody was willing to talk if needed. My mother had light brown hair, with a tint of blonde and red. She still flaunted her modern sixties shag, if that makes any sense, and her clothes were usually stylish, even for our generation. It made her look youthful. She stood about five foot three and was very thin, which is surprising for a lady in her late forties. Most ladies at that age have a potbelly that hangs over their knees and boobs that sag over their potbelly. So I considered her fairly lucky. But her one problem was that she smoked far too much, always sucking the life out of those Marlboro lights and exhaling only after her lungs could no longer withstand the torture of the Indian peace pipe tradition. But everybody has a hobby, and I suppose smoking was hers. You can't condemn her for it. Just have to tell her the disadvantages and let her handle it.

"People, people, hear ye, hear ye. I have a story to tell which you all might find interesting." Everybody tuned into radio station Steve Nichols. "I met one of the campaign managers to Bill Clinton, who supposedly worked for him at the time he was running for governor. I was beyond intoxication when I began talking to him, so the conversation started off something like, 'How's it feel to be talking to a future President?' I asked him this as I was putting my arm around his date for the night."

"You're even a male slut when it comes to other men's women, aren't ya Steve?" Kristie added another statement of jealousy, which sent Steve into an outburst of one of his patented cocky laughs.

"What . . . What? I had no idea she was with him . . . Usually when I'm with a girl, she's by my side, but this girl was two seats away from him and she was looking at me the whole time."

"It's possible that you were drunk to the point of hallucination," I said, raising my eyebrows.

"I was beyond the point of hallucination Doug, there's no

contesting that," Steve answered with another cocky grin. "But as I was saying, this guy then went on with a reply of, 'Well how's it feel talking to a past campaign manager of Bill Clinton?' He sounded Italian or something. He had one of those mobster guinea voices. Or maybe it was more mobster Sicilian like!" He said this just to make my sister and me mad. He knew we were Sicilian and he always made jokes about our great, great, great grandmother having sex with a black man . . . and how that gene is still being passed down through the generations, leaving us to inherit that black gene. He got the idea from a movie, *True Romance*.

Steve continued, "After he made this statement, I just kind of sat there. I took a swig of beer because I was dumbfounded that this idiot would have been proud to have worked for Bill Clinton. And although I knew he was lying, I still wanted to humor him some. So I asked him why he wasn't still working for him. This is his answer, 'Well, I-I . . . uh,' he kept stuttering and tripping over his words, 'I was fired because word got out that I was smoking marijuana.' Once again, I was completely dumbfounded at his mere idiocy, until I finally had to tell him what I had been thinking the whole time I was talking to him. I told him, 'First of all, I know you weren't a campaign manager for Bill Clinton because you're a drunken idiot who could never get a job in the political field. Second of all, I can't believe you would have been proud to have worked for Bill Clinton and then made up the pathetic excuse that he fired you due to smoking marijuana. Why didn't you just tell the media you didn't inhale as your so-called buddy Bill Clinton did? Now for the third statement before I leave you to wallow in your sorriness, I'm going to leave without your woman so that you'll have somebody to comfort you in your pathetic world of dreams.'"

Everybody's mouth was open in shock, unable to believe that Steve had been so cruel to somebody who was probably trying to make himself better only because he knew he was worse. But I couldn't blame Steve for what he did. People shouldn't try and be something that they're not. And they definitely shouldn't lie about the person that they are. It only makes them look like the pathetic piece of work that they really are. Not that people should be judged by another, but it's distressing to see a person who has a lot of potential—and everybody has potential—just throw their life away into a black hole of nothingness.

I remember a conversation Steve and I had in one of our rare moments of sobriety. It started off with me saying that Steve sometimes called people worthless, and I argued his statement by saying that nobody was worthless. And I didn't see what gave him the right to call somebody that. I asked him what made him better than the next person. He talked his way out of it again and explained that he didn't think any life was worthless. He said there was no such thing as a waste of life. Everybody has God-given talents in which they could build a foundation for their life and create success from those talents. Then he went on to explain that there is such a thing as a waste of talents, and because they don't use those talents, they are wasting away a better life. And he's right. Some people with amazing abilities don't use what they have, and they just waste their abilities away on drugs or laziness.

"Good Steve . . . the poor fella probably went home and hanged himself," his dad said in a 'half-joking, yet trying to teach his children morals' way.

Steve began again, "You know what I find humorous though, is the fact that when I stumbled out of my chair to find someone intelligent to talk to, his woman grabbed my arm and asked if I wanted a drink. So you can imagine the kind of abuse these people take. I'm sure my saying that isn't the worse thing he's ever heard."

Everybody was surprised. Steve had a legitimate point. A person is basically treated how they let themselves be treated, so I guess this guy let himself be abused. It's not everybody else's job to make sure that people treat him properly.

"Very interesting story Steve, but I'm afraid we have to get going. I have to make these college kids a home cooked meal for once." My mother had the right idea to get us back home. Brockport food was tasty, but there's nothing like a home cooked meal after having greasy college food for so long.

"Hey Doug, sometime when Kristie and your mom aren't around, I'll have to tell you all my stories about fraternity parties and the women who come to them."

This time Kristie showed no jealousy. "You're not the only one who's been hitting it big with the opposite sex!"

"I thought the electric fence sent shock waves through my body . . . the crude remarks between the two of you is twice the shock." Jeff was right. For two people who used to be so much in love, they sure had a lot of differences to settle if that love was ever to occur again.

Chapter Seven

"Hey Doug, are you going out tonight?" he asked with one arm holding himself up against the side of the door and the other one hanging down by his hip with a joint in his hand. He was always high or drunk, basically always on some sort of drug to blur away his life. His name was Brian. He lived right across the hall from me at my college dorm. A lot of girls thought he was a 'hottie'. But they all said they could never date him because all he cared about was drugs. Like I said, everybody has their own hobby or something to relax them, and I guess you really can't condemn them for it, although it is many times very detrimental to their health.

"You know what I always do on the weekend, Brian. Go out to Happy Hour, get drunk at the bars, and stumble home trying to act sober past the cops so they don't pick me up for a fake I.D., and then pass out on my bed after a failed attempt at trying to get a honey."

"Offer 'em some of this shit and they'll come around," Brian struggled to say as a big white smiled flared out at the thought of another joint.

"Ha, ha, not a bad idea . . . but I prefer my ladies to be alcoholics over drug addicts. Jus Ki, Jus Ki." I unlocked my door only to find out that I had locked it again. My roommate got home from class before me and he sometimes unlocked the door, but closed it. I always forgot to check if it was locked before entering, so I would sometimes lock it back up trying to open it. I finally got in, but my roomie Matt was not there. I figured he was probably down the hall or something trying to pick up one of the honeys down there. "Ah, the advantages of a coed dorm," I thought to myself, whispering it because nobody else was in the room. I sprawled myself out on my comfortable bed, closed my eyes just glad to finally have some peace for the day.

"Doug, Doug, are you in there?" Disappointed that an attempt was being made to disrupt my peace, I remained quiet with my eyes shut, just hoping for her to go away. But she entered my room and peaked around the corner. "Doug, if you're asleep, wake up. I have something important to tell you."

"Heather, this better be important . . . you come in here far too many times and disrupt my rest with your nonexistent troubles." She looked a little baffled, so I threw in a joke to make it sound like the whole statement was in jest. "How do you expect me to stay up long enough to get drunk if I don't rest for my hard night?" I squeezed out a little snort of laughter, and she smiled back.

"Well, this is really important Doug. T.J. left a message with us; I have no idea why he left it with us. But he said that one of your good friends had gotten in a really bad car accident and to call him back immediately." Her expression changed to complete seriousness and the tone in her voice sounded anxious. She had her trouble with a friend dying in a car accident, so she was probably worried that the same tragedy was going to befall me.

"Aw, don't worry about it Heather. T.J. said it, now come on. I'm sure it's no big deal. You know how he always makes things more dramatic than they really are. It's probably someone that I barely even know." I really wasn't too worried. He did many times make a situation more dramatic. Like when he got injured in a sport, he would talk and complain about it for the next week, even if it was just a scratch. Or when he was telling a story about a fight between him and his girlfriend, he would make it sound like she was devastated and he nearly demolished her self-worth.

But I picked up the phone anyway and dialed in my pin number to reach T.J. Everybody had to have a pin number to make calls out so that the college would know who to charge the phone bill to. It was a pain for me though because I didn't call out too often, so I always had to pull my paper out of a tight, white envelope to see what my pin number was. But for some reason, I remembered it at that moment and was relieved that I didn't have to find that envelope again. I dialed in the nine digit number followed by T.J.'s phone number, and waited while the phone rang three times, whispering to myself, "If it's that serious, why the hell doesn't the bastard pick up the phone?"

"Hello." Somebody finally picked up. It was T.J.'s sister. I could tell by her voice.

"Hello Jill, is T.J. there?"

"No . . . I thought he was up there with you!"

"Dude, Jill, the kid comes up to party every weekend . . . we couldn't let him up here again."

"Oh, you haven't found out yet?"

I didn't like the sound of that question. I felt acid release into my stomach causing a burning sensation and a ticklish feeling at the same time. My voice sounded a little jittery as I spoke, just waiting for the inevitable story to be told to me. "Wha- . . . What do you mean? He said something about an accident, but I just threw it off as no big worry." Jill then breathed a big sigh as I patiently waited to hear what happened. There was a dead silence in the air, and my world had stopped in place, waiting for the news. She finally muttered out the story, explaining in disbelief something that I thought never would or could happen to one of our E.B. gang members.

"It's Jeff . . ." My heart fell down my throat into the fiery acid of my stomach and just burned there waiting to here the rest of the story. The blood in my veins froze up more with every word she spoke and my mind struggled for control. "He got in a bad car accident!" The word "accident" echoed through my head and rang in my ears like a high-pitched scream in the darkest tunnel, sending me into waves of misunderstanding of what couldn't be understood. "He was injured the worst. He was with three other kids. One was Jay Vandermeer and I'm not sure who the other two were. They said that Jay may never be able to run cross-country again and they said that Jeff might not even survive. He's in the Intensive Care Unit at Strong Memorial Hospital in Rochester if you guys want to go and see him."

I could only speak one phrase in my state of shock. "Holy shit . . ." The words came out slowly, but surly. I heard Jill talking to me in the background, but I don't remember what she said. It was one of those times in your life where you block out everything, even part of your memory. I don't even remember how I got off the phone with her. I just remember hanging it up and standing there, frozen with my hand on the receiver, until I finally heard the annoying 'beep, beep' that always came when the phone was off the hook too long. It sounded so freaky at that moment, like it was meant to be placed there. It was one of those directed scenes in a movie, where everything in life, everything that the performer had worked and fought for, had just come to a complete dead-end. Something far more important, something far worse, had just changed everything. And that is where the movie ends. It is the part followed by the beeping of the receiver and the screen fading out into the color black, leaving the viewer with only the sound of the beep for about thirty seconds until the names of the producers roll upward across the screen. But this was no movie. There were no producers to end the production and make everything go back to normal, the way it once was. The only producer was fate.

The word stood out to me at that moment. It was imprinted onto the wall of my imagination in large, black letters. My eyes could see it clearly, as they were fixed at the top of my eyelids, reaching for my eyebrows. They were gazing at that director called fate with a death cold stare. "One hell of a movie," I thought to myself. This time, I didn't whisper the words out loud, for the lone reason that I was insane with painstaking confusion. I struggled to escape my momentous stare, in case somebody entered the room. It was finally broken by the call of my name.

"Doug . . ." I turned sharply to see the sight of Marcea standing in the doorway. She lived right down the hall from me. "How's your friend little love bunny?" We always used little pet names for each other, just joking around. But I wasn't in the mood for bantering right then. I felt like I would never be in the mood again. But I put up a front. I wasn't lying about who I was. I was just lying to myself about how I felt about the whole situation.

"Actually he's not doing too well." Just then Heather entered my room and plopped herself onto my bed without permission. But I kept speaking. "He's in the Intensive Care Unit right now, and I guess they aren't even sure if he'll survive."

Heather picked her head up from my pillow with a look of terror on her face. She was probably reliving her past trauma through my situation. Marcea did what she always did when she didn't know what else to say, she repeated what I had said. "Aren't even sure if he'll live," saying it almost as if she hadn't understood me the first time.

I just shrugged my shoulders and simply replied, "I guess." I said it fluently, like I didn't care. I said it like he wasn't even that close of a friend and that I barely knew the guy. But he was a close friend and I knew him well. So well that I couldn't let it hurt. My heart turned to stone right then—comparable to the lifeless stone that I once stood upon at Kistner Concrete. One of those that could never be softened by anybody but yourself, and could not be broken because it could no longer love. And it could no longer cry, even if it wanted to. But it could still feel. I could deny my feelings, but they were still there . . . they were there deep inside my gut where I had pushed them all down to hide.

Marcea just shook her head, saying, "I'm so sorry," and then left my room for lack of anything better to say. Heather was still there, looking at me with that look of terror, and also a look of amazement.

"What's wrong? You act like you've just seen a ghost." I added in a little chuckle to spice up the moment with a little acted happiness.

"Maybe I'm looking at one Doug . . ." She paused briefly in hopes of getting some sort of confused reaction out of me. But I remained still, at ease with my eyes fixed onto hers, almost challenging her to say more. "You act like you don't even care. Is there anything in there?"

"Oh, of course I care, but there's not much that I can really do about it . . ." I paused momentarily trying to reassure myself that there really wasn't much I could do about it, so I shouldn't worry about it. "Besides, I'm sure he'll be alright." I smiled and turned my head toward my desk, looking through the pages of my communications book, wondering if there was any way to get to the hospital to see my buddy Jeff. I heard footsteps prance behind me and looked onto my bed to see that Heather had left the room. I was all alone in my violent world, wondering what the next deviant surprise would be. I turned my head toward the ceiling and said a little prayer for him to be all right, and then I waited there. I just waited for life to take its course. And then the phone rang, this time startling me out of deep thought.

"Hello."

"Hi Doug, this is Kristie . . . I don't think I'll be going out tonight. I have other plans."

"Like what, going to see Jeff?"

She waited a moment before speaking. Kind of like she was surprised that I knew. "Yeah, Steve asked me to keep it from you . . . how'd you know?"

I sighed and spoke. "T.J. called me and said that a good friend had gotten hurt. I called back and talked to his sister, only to find out it was Jeff."

"I can't believe it . . . Steve asked me not to tell you because he didn't want to upset you."

I had to put on my macho front, and act like it didn't bother me the least little bit. "Oh no, I'm alright. I'm glad I found out. I'd hate to be left in the dark on something like this. Hell, if he's not gonna make it, then I'd like to see him before he plunders." I spoke so heartlessly, but I felt in control of my emotions then. But I wasn't in control. I was a tower of outrage ready to explode. A tower beginning in my stomach and building layer upon layer of itself, up through my esophagus and leading straight toward my brain.

"Look, why don't we get together and find a way to get to the hospital to see him. We'll call around for a bus or something." We made our agreement and I hung up the phone, threw my new winter jacket around my shoulders and made a run for the door. I heard Heather behind me asking where I was going, but I didn't answer her. I wasn't much in the mood to talk to somebody like her. Somebody who would tell me all of her problems when I really felt like dealing with my own for the time being.

I walked through the brisk, autumn air on that evening in October. Large flurries of snow came fluttering down upon my head, giving my hair a natural wash. The snowflakes didn't come down in abundance. They came down slowly, one at a time, trying to find a place on earth where they could settle. Those snowflakes were so peaceful. They were having the time of their lives, flying through the refrigerated air on earth. They were seeing all kinds of sites. But as they fell on me, they fell on a grim site. As I glanced up into the air and caught a glimpse of the snowflakes, I noticed that the furry headed angels were laughing at me, almost mocking me. Their fully designed faces were betraying my dismal situation with their laughter and fun. And in their world of peace, they had no time to do anything but taunt me with their luxury. A snowflake fluttered down onto my eye, leaving a slushy trail in my lid and causing me to squint and clear away the gushy mess. After clearing my eye, I looked up at the snowflakes again—but this time, only to see them in their peace, living in their heavenly world. So I was alone to ponder over what could be done, which was nothing. Nothing but to hope for the best and expect the worst.

I finally reached the door leading into my sister's suite room. I opened the door to find her making phone calls to an information line, asking about transportation leading to Strong Memorial Hospital in Rochester.

"Yes . . . no . . . yes . . . so you don't have any buses leading to Rochester tonight." I could hear the loud voice of the operator on the other end. It was one of those annoying, squeaky voices with a snotty attitude. "O.K., thank you and goodbye."

She hung up the phone in frustration and let out a rush of air. "I don't know how we're going to get there. No buses out of Brockport tonight. There's a bunch of snow warnings and they're scared to make any unnecessary trips."

"This isn't an unnecessary trip!" I burst out. Kristie looked at me helplessly. "I don't believe this. We can't even get out of this damn town when we want to." Right as I spoke, I heard the voice of T.J. behind me.

"I've got a place for you to go." I turned around, happy to see him. "So I see you two already found out about Jeff." His voice was a little depressed. Both my sister and I nodded our heads. All three of us stood there for a moment, staring at the ground, waiting for our next action to take place.

"Hey T.J., how'd you get up here?"

"Well, I drove my station wagon so we could go and see Jeff. You guys ready?" I nodded my head again, now aware of the reason why T.J. had come up for us. So we could all see Jeff together. Without another word, we zipped up our jackets and made our way to his '82 Malibu. The car didn't handle too well in the snow. The back tires would sometimes slide around and fishtail. We all made jokes about how we would probably get into an accident on the way there to see Jeff, trying to make light of the situation of course.

Getting to the hospital wasn't as easy as we had first thought. We had no idea which road to start on, until T.J. asked some mid-twenties lady at the Brockport gas station, who shot us in the right direction. Then as we entered Rochester, the city that the hospital was in, we couldn't quite find the hospital. We asked some lady on a side street which way to go, but she seemed paranoid and told us to look in the phone book. We assumed she was a little wacky. We then ended up at another hospital, in which I went in to ask the attendant how to get to our destination. I realized it was a mental hospital when I got up to the porch, only to see some longhaired guy slap his girlfriend on the ass, and then say, "We can talk about that a little later, ha? Ha, ha, ha!" She laughed one of those psychotic laughs and then walked away with his hand on her ass. I made my daring entrance into the mental hospital anyway, as it was my only source of information. The security guard at the front desk directed me to the right street, so we left that dungeon of psycho recruits. The trip there was kind of funny in a way. It cheered us up from the depressing thought of what was to come. It's strange, because when you're in a hurry to do something or to get somewhere, it seems like the most precarious situations slow you down. But we were a determined group and we found our destination.

All our joking and laughter stopped once we pulled into the parking lot. We had to take a bus to the hospital because the hospital-parking garage was under construction and the place we parked was about a mile away. But our determination kept us moving, and so did the bus. It pulled into Strong Memorial Hospital, and not a word was said between the three of us until we walked inside, and up to the front desk.

"Can you tell us where Jeff Nichols is?" I asked the nurse hoping that she wouldn't give us one of those stubborn lines that we wouldn't be able to see him because we weren't family. And she didn't. She didn't even have to look up the room number and told us straight out.

"He's on the second floor, room 1204. I know it by heart now, so many people have asked me." She made a slight attempt at a joke, so we all just let out one of those fake laughs to make the nurse feel better, and then made a mad dash for the elevator to catch it before the door locked us out. We jumped in the crowded elevator of about ten people, when the maximum was ten. But the door closed before anybody could object. I smelled a distinct odor coming from the man behind me. It was actually one of those nursing home odors, where it smells like every one of the patients forgot to put on their deodorant for the day. But we weren't in a nursing home; we were in a hospital. It didn't matter though. I didn't like the smell of either. A hospital odor reminds me of pain and agony. You can almost smell the odor of people suffering in the air. I especially didn't like it now that my friend was the one who was suffering, not some fifty-eighth step relative who I barely even knew.

The elevator finally made a stop. I looked up and noticed that it was not our floor. We were supposed to stop on the second floor, and for some reason, the elevator had skipped over our floor and went straight to the third. A family of Puerto Ricans walked out, about five in all, which left a lot more room for everybody else to breathe. Then the elevator made its way up again, this time to the fourth floor, which let two more people out.

"Why the hell did it just skip over the second floor?" I burst out in sudden frustration at not being able to see my buddy. T.J. shook his head. Then the deep voice of an African American male sounded behind me.

"Probably 'cause no one pressed it!" His tone was a little snotty, but he made me realize that nobody had even pressed the button to the second floor yet. So I forcefully pressed my finger on the button and repeatedly pushed it for about thirty seconds. I could tell the man behind me was getting annoyed, but I didn't care. I was frustrated and in a great hurry. The other three people in the elevator got off on the eighth floor. The man gave me a slight nudge as he walked by, probably unknowingly. I paid no attention and pressed the close door button, then relaxed as the elevator made its way down to our second floor destination.

"Things seem pretty serious now," T.J. remarked from the

back of the descending prison we were in. I knew exactly what he meant. We didn't even know what we were about to see, but we knew it would probably be one of the most unpleasant experiences of our lives. One thought I distinctly remember was what I enjoyed most about being in that elevator. It was the fact that it was postponing the inevitable sight. It was my little stoppage of time, the point at which I could relax my inner self so as to prepare for the sight of the injured hero.

The elevator door opened and I was faced with the sight of five impatient people trying to get in. My sister, T.J., and I gave each other a quick smirk to add some cheer to the situation, and then walked out of the elevator. We turned the corner with confusion, not knowing where room 1204 was. But as we turned another corner, we noticed a large quantity of people standing in the hospital hallway near the Intensive Care Unit, with eyes bloodshot red from tears and cheeks blushed with sorrow.

Kristie began speaking with a soft tone. "This must be it. Where's the parent- . . ." She stopped abruptly. I looked over toward the hallway of tears, and saw Jeff's mother walking out of Jeff's hospital room.

Her walk was without poise and confidence, unlike the way it usually was. Her face was white almost like she'd just seen a ghost, and her eyes were wet with the flooding of tears. I believe you can tell a lot by a person's eyes. Her eyes didn't only tell that she was sad and heartbroken, but it also told of the drowning of her world as she knew it. A world in which there would be no man named Noah to come and carry her along on his ark, but one in which she would have to build her own canoe and paddles. One in which she would have to make every movement of the paddle by herself, against torrential waves that are far too overbearing for even the strongest to guide themselves through.

She staggered over to Kristie, and just clamped onto her, falling with faithful allegiance to Kristie's strength. Kristie held onto her, and cried with her. They let out only a minute portion of their feelings, so as to save themselves from the devastation of agony. I could hear Kathy mumbling about how she was so scared, about how it never should have happened to somebody like him.

I could only stand there and watch, helpless to do anything but grin and bear it. In a way though, I understood it, just not to the extent that Kathy did. I thought back to the times when I would leave for a party, or when I left for college. I thought of my mother's reactions or responses to my farewells as I walked out of the house. My mother was **one** of the most loving human beings in the world. I say she was only **one** of them because the majority of mothers are such lovable people, with so much of a guiding hand for their children that I swear God is sure to have created the 'chicken before the egg'. After all the hatched egg would never have survived without the chicken, its mother. I once realized, when mothers say 'I love you', they don't say another word until you say it back to them. It's because they want to know that all the love and caring they've given their children has produced a loveable child all the same, to pass on the immaculate emotion throughout the generations. Otherwise, their life would be unbearable. Most certainly, they love their children with all their heart and soul. When one of those children is leaving, lost or injured to some aspect of life, they most certainly bare the brunt of the hurt. And the pain and anguish that Kathy felt at the news of Jeff's car crash must have felt like relentless needle pricks stabbing at her heart.

I looked for somebody to talk to so that I could find out what the situation was, so I could find out whether or not my buddy was even alive. I noticed Steve standing with some relatives, still holding his composure and talking to his relatives about what the present situation was. I walked over to join the discussion. He saw me coming over and greeted me with a respectful handshake.

"How are you, Doug?"

"I think the appropriate question is, how are you?"

"About as good as can be expected at a moment like this, I suppose."

I hesitated to bring up the question that I was sure he had been asked so many times already, but I couldn't resist the temptation of curiosity. "So how is the bugger?"

There was a slight pause and then a sigh from Steve to pass some time before answering. I knew by his reaction that he would not give me a soothing reply. "Well first of all, the neurologists aren't even too sure what the situation is. They even admitted that nobody knows too much about the human brain, not even them. But they said that there is no way of knowing right now whether or not he'll live. And they said that if he does live, that there would probably be irreversible damage. They gave the family many scenarios of what has happened with other accident victims when they were injured like Jeff . . ."

I waited for a moment as he tucked in his shirt and took off his glasses to think more clearly. "Well, what's happened with other people who had injuries such as Jeff's?" I planted my body solid in its position to brace myself for his answer, at the same time just hoping that it would be an appeasement.

"Well, most of the cases, the victim either died or spent his life in a coma. But he said he's heard of cases where people have fought out of a coma and lived normal lives . . ."

"But he's just never seen one?" I replied, half-asking, half-finishing his sentence.

"Well yes, those were basically his words."

I walked back toward T.J. so that I could tell him the news. He was waiting patiently, expecting nothing better than the worse, just hoping for more. I told him what I had heard, and his hopeful expression kind of drooped down, losing some of its existence. Then his eyes widened and I looked behind me to see the face of Jeff's father, Gary Nichols, waiting to accept our proposal of helping in any way that we could.

"Good to see you boys . . . how are ya?" His voice was still relaxed, but I noticed that it was different in some way. Maybe it sounded somewhat battle torn. Not really worried though. You could see the worry in his eyes, but his voice held that emotion secretly in its voice box.

"I'm doin' alright. Going to G.C.C. now." T.J. talked to him as if nothing had even happened.

"Playing baseball, are ya?" I was amazed at Gary's ease at such a time. I was able to tell that he was hurting inside, but he still put others before himself, always interested to see how their lives were coming along. That's how the whole family was—always considerate of others while putting themselves second to everyone else.

"How about you, Doug? Are you playing baseball?"

"No . . . no . . . I plan to start in the spring. I thought I'd try the whole college scene out first and see how things work out." Saying this made me think of Jeff once again. I remember talk about how he was supposed to go to college, either down south to play baseball, or maybe even to Brockport if the situation would allow. But it seemed as if the situation wasn't allowing. It was throwing curveballs with rocks and building a mountain too high to climb.

"You boys can see him in a second when his grandparents get out. We'll go in there with you." T.J. and I held a look of astonishment as he once again put us before anyone else.

"Mr. Nichols, if it's a problem, we'll stay out he- . . ."

"Oh no T.J., it's no problem. You two have just as much need to see him as everybody else."

Three of the four grandparents came walking out. Norman Nichols was in a back room. His forgetfulness caused him trouble in understanding what was happening. Everybody told him that Jeff had gotten in an accident, and he didn't really seem to understand the seriousness in it. Most of the family agreed that it was probably better that way.

The grandparents looked like everybody else who had come out of Jeff's room. Battle torn and saddened by the gruesome thought of what had happened, and of what was still yet to come.

Gary Nichols set his hand on my shoulder and nodded toward the room, guiding us in the right direction. Steve met up beside T.J. and me, with Kristie wrapped in his arm. We all made our way toward the ICU with cautious strides, as if our weight would cause damage to Jeff's condition. I remember walking slowly into that room, trying to restrain myself from entering, yet at the same time anxious to see what everybody else was crying over.

I entered the room to the sound of beeping from the mechanisms all around his body. He had a ventilator to keep him breathing, with a tube driven into his throat to allow oxygen into his lungs. I noticed the mechanical movement of his chest, moving up and down to the sound of every beep on the ventilator. He was a machine himself, trying to get out and be human. I looked at his scarred up face, beaten and scratched up from the window glass, but still saw the red birthmark that held itself strongly in its place on his cheek. The same birthmark that had been the center of much ridicule, and also the same birthmark that stuck with him in his most troublesome endeavor. It was still Jeff I saw in that hospital bed, but not the same Jeff. Not the same Jeff that I rode into some evergreen trees with. Not the same Jeff who used to run cross-country, play basketball, and baseball. And certainly not the same one who used to smoke cigars and drink malt liquors with us down in my basement. He was a new Jeff in a new life of raw dealings. He would now have to face challenges far greater than trying to be the last one from throwing up due to intoxication. He would never be able to run again, shoot again, or hit again. He was and always will lay in his bed, always thinking about how great it was to do all the things that normal, healthy kids are able to do, yet never being able to do it himself.

"They said he probably won't even live. If he makes it through the next twenty-four hours, then he's lucky." A voice whispered at my side. It echoed throughout my eardrum, cascading itself into my brain and forcing me to realize the seriousness of what had come into everybody's life. T.J. had just talked quietly with the doctor and found out some interesting and tragic facts about my compadre. It hit me all at once, almost knocking me into a coma myself and nearly bringing a blush of anger to my cheeks. My buddy was facing death, and there wasn't a damn thing that I could do about it. Not a damn thing, except pray and hope. Hope . . . a word that never seems to get you anywhere, but never fails to bring you somewhere.

Kathy grabbed a dry washcloth and dipped it into a bucket full of ice water. I watched as she squeezed the cloth so that not one droplet of water was retained in it. Her hands looked so helpless, yet struggled with courage to help her ailing son. She placed the washcloth on his legs, and then reached into a cupboard to grab some more.

"It's to keep his temperature down." I looked up and noticed that Gary was talking to me. He must have known that I was confused by my look of bewilderment.

"Isn't there a possibility of frostbite," I asked, first looking at Gary and then glancing toward the doctor for an answer.

"Probably only if it's on for long periods of time . . . besides, when faced with the situation he's in . . . frostbite is the least of his worries." The response seemed kind of cold-hearted to me. But at least the doctor was honest; I had to give him credit for that. He never tried to falsify hope. He told the situation as it was, no matter how terrible.

I saw Kristie with my peripheral vision. She covered Steve's hand with her own. He had two fingers on Jeff's wrist. Whether to feel his pulse or just a touch of love and security, I don't know. But he was there for Jeff as a brother is always there for his own blood. He was a block of concrete standing there, phased by nothing, but brewing a beer of sadness in his stomach.

Kristie was staring into Steve's eyes while holding tears in her own. You could see that she loved him, and she loved Jeff as a second brother.

Kathy was whispering in Jeff's ear. Words of encouragement, anything to keep him fighting and to take away his worries. Gary Nichols held on to Jeff's other hand, slightly massaging it and increasing the flow of warm blood throughout Jeff's body. T.J. was standing behind me. I don't know what he was thinking or doing. But I know that he remained nearly motionless. I couldn't even hear his breathing. I also remained motionless. I wanted to say something. Maybe a little joke to lift his spirits. Or a little crack about the spot on his cheek to increase his hope. But I felt awkward. Nobody knew whether or not he could hear anybody. So I didn't speak. It was better that way. I just watched him struggle with every breath. But it wasn't him struggling; it was the machine that he was attached to. An I.V. needle poked through the top of his hand to supply him with necessary water and nutrients. A tracheotomy was jammed impeccably into his throat to supply him with oxygen, surrounded by dying skin flushed with open wounds of red blood. And ice cold, white cloths covered his naked body to keep his temperature at or below a hundred degrees. A large, stitched up gash covered the right side of his head, leaving a flat indent.

"What's the indent in his head from?" I didn't know whether to ask in front of Jeff, or to wait until we were outside the room. I spoke hesitantly, but once the question started coming out, I continued fluently.

Gary Nichols came closer to me and whispered in my ear. "They performed surgery and cut out a section of his skull to make room for the swelling." He went on, sending volts of anguish through me. "If they didn't cut out part of his skull, then the swelling would have been too large for what his skull could withstand."

I nodded my head, letting Mr. Nichols know that I had heard him, and that I didn't want to hear anymore. The nurse then entered the room. She was quite a pretty girl. She had long, brown hair that stretched down to the middle of her back, and had quite a bubbly attitude. "Y'all will have to leave now, except fo' the family. We don't have enough room for y'all." I looked at her and stared her straight in the eyes. She just smiled at me. I stared because I saw the beauty in her, and it is that same beauty in her that Jeff would probably never again be able to see. He was a boy who never had a serious relationship in his life—never had a love—and now, he probably never would. As strange as it might seem to think of a problem so small compared to the seriousness of what had happened, but it makes sense. Love is meant to be one of the finer pleasures in life. And I could only think of how he would never be able to experience that pleasure. And love isn't the only thing he would probably never be able to do again. He couldn't experience happiness because now he only knew sadness, if he could even feel emotion at all. He was a prisoner locked up with the rest of the innocent victims, who were all wrongly convicted, and were now unwillingly sacrificing their lives for the crimes which others had committed.

I walked out of the room, and heard the nurse shut the door behind me. Steve was allowed to stay in there if he wanted to, but came out to talk to all the new visitors, or even people who had been there awhile but still had not received an explanation with all the mass confusion. I don't know if I looked like everybody else who had entered the room, whether or not my face was like a ghost's, nor did I care. If I didn't look horrified, I sure felt it in my stomach.

I walked into a dreary room where Jeff's parents would be sleeping for the night. All the family members who were able to make it to the hospital were there in that room. Steve was outside where there was a telephone.

"Steve's still wheeling and dealing on the phone . . . calling his college advisor and trying to settle things," his grandmother said with pride. Steve was calling his college to see if he could make arrangements to take some time off and still be able to maintain his 4.0 GPA. I went in the room and sat down, with Kristie finding a seat beside me. I listened to the sobs and tears. I watched as his fully bearded Uncle Doug walked in to see Jeff as an indestructible image of manhood, and come out a reconstructed image of tears. I heard the reciting of prayers, and prayed along with them. Then I heard stories of what had happened, and who was to blame.

I was told that Jeff's friend had only yielded to a stop sign, meanwhile an ambulance was driving about eighty miles per hour down Sweetland Road, on its way to another accident. It hit the car, full of four kids, directly on the side, striking Jeff the hardest. Nobody knew where the fault should lie. It wasn't a time for thinking about lawsuits anyway, but more a time of praying for the life of a loved one. The worst story I heard though, of what I recall, was that the driver of the ambulance felt no remorse whatsoever. He felt that it was not his fault, and therefore distanced himself from any responsibility to the accident. I was disgusted when I heard that. A live human being was facing death at the worst, and a life in a wheelchair at the best, and all the driver could say is that he felt no remorse. I've been told society keeps getting worse. I don't believe that, I really don't. I'm somewhat idealistic when it comes to what is really becoming of the world. But when I hear something like that, I realize what the real problem in the world is. It's the lack of caring and deserving love that people used to give for one another. And if not that, at least a sense of respect, enough to say that they are sorry, even if it's not their fault. Just to apologize for the fact that they were involved, rather than to place the blame on something else so as to take the guilt off themselves. Such people are cowards if they cannot admit to a wrongdoing, but heroes when they try and make up for it.

But there was no making up for what had happened. There were tears and sorrow all around, a feeling that there might never again be happiness within the family. And there might never again be the same happiness within myself. One of my buddies had been seriously injured in a war, in the battle of life. And all the struggles that anybody might endure could not bring him out of his suffering.

I walked into a well-lit room across the hall. It was smaller, but was furnished with nicer chairs and tables and flowery wallpaper border that seemed to want to put one in a better mood. So I sat down on the couch there, first by myself, and then I was graced with the presence of a good friend of the family, Corrinne. Her parents were good friends of Jeff's family, and she was in love with Jeff. She always had been and probably always will be. She looked very troubled and shocked, but still held hope in her eyes.

"How are ya, Doug?"

"As Steve would say, about as good as can be expected at a time like this." I composed a fake grin, a closed grin, to try and show a little promise. She returned it with the same closed grin and then sat down. After not saying a word for almost five minutes, she finally came out with something.

"So how's college? Do you get pretty drunk and high up there all the time?"

I was a little surprised at her comment as I have never been a big pot smoker. I never really saw the purpose in it. Every person I've ever seen that had a near addiction to it, if that's possible, always turned out to be lazy and didn't do anything with their life no matter how many talents they had. "I haven't been spending my time getting high, but as for drinking, that's a different story. In fact, that's a whole story in itself." She smiled, this time with a more open smile, and a little more realistic, though I could still tell it was forced. Then she brought back the mood that we were both experiencing, but too afraid to show or talk about.

"So how do you think he'll turn out?"

"How do you think?" I quickly reversed the question to take the attention off me.

"I'm hopeful. He's a fighter, right? Life isn't that cruel. I don't think it will be cruel enough to take the life of an innocent kid. Nor could it be cruel enough to turn him into a comatose . . ." She drooped down for a moment and then spoke again. "I think it's just setting him up to make a heroic comeback." She let out an even wider smile when she said that, and this time even more realistic. But I could still tell it was fake. Just a smile to reassure herself, maybe to help her believe that what she was saying about the heroic comeback was actually true. I smiled back, also to reassure myself that something good would come out of this. Something good always comes out of bad. At least that's what I had told myself. Now I had no choice but to wait and see if my belief would bear fruit.

"So what do you think, Doug?" She once again brought up the question that I had before so quickly changed. But this time, after a few moments, I answered it.

"I'm hopeful. You're right. He's a fighter. Always has been and always will be. I'm just waiting for him to sit up in that bed and say, 'Jus Ki, Jus Ki.'"

Corrinne broke out in laughter at the comment, and then stumbled out with some words of her own. "You, Jeff, and T.J. always were big on that 'Jus Ki' kick, weren't you? It's like you have your own little clan of the three stooges. After you three beat up on each other, you just keep saying, 'Jus Ki, Jus Ki.'"

She was right in a way. We three did use those words a lot. We had a gang of five, but it was kind of like us three were a gang within a gang. The 'Jus Ki' gang. We all had used the words after just about every sentence. We even have a picture of us three together. It's a picture at my graduation party. The three of us standing there together—T.J. on the left side, me on the right, and Jeff in the middle. Jeff was the tall one standing there with a goofy smile on his face, and I was the shortest, looking like a freshman in high school when I was really on my way to being a freshman in college. And then there was T.J., with a stupid, drunken look on his face as he was staring straight into the camera like he wanted to fight the photographer. The type of look that an Irishman always has when he's half sloshed. The background was mostly dark, bringing more attention to the E.B. boys. The grass was cluttered beneath our feet, showing the country life in all its glory, and the country boys in all their glory. The thought of the picture made me happy for the moment. But the entrance of Corrinne's mother, followed by T.J., and then my beautiful sister, Kristie, soon interrupted my happiness.

<>The 'Jus Ki' Gang of the E.B. Gang<>

"Where'd all you people come from?" I asked mainly 'cause I was surprised that they knew the room was there.

"The other room was too depressing. We had to go somewhere to relax." Kristie was such an intelligent girl. She was a strong girl and knew how to relieve stress in different ways than drinking away her sorrows or secluding herself from the world.

We all sat there for a while. Then Corrinne's mother spoke up. She asked the question that everybody had been asking all night. "So how is everybody?"

We all gave her that fake smile that everybody had been practicing all night. She repeated her question, so we repeated our smiles. Then Grandma Nichols came walking in, with tears in her eyes.

"There's a seat over here Grandma Nichols." Corrinne's mother called her Grandma Nichols even though she wasn't related to the family. Pretty much everybody who knew her called her that. She was just the perfect caring grandmother, so everybody thought of her as their own.

She sat down, sort of plopped down on the couch like she had no energy left to move herself even a hair more. She was crying; not really hysterically crying, but enough so we could see the tears. She began sobbing out a story. Her voice was scratchy, which I expected was caused from the body releasing all its moisture through tears. "I just found out about Todd. He is so young. He keeps asking his mom . . . is Jeff gonna die?" More tears flowed down her cheek when she said the word die. She was careful to say it, almost as if she said it too loud, that it might come true. So she spoke it in a quiet squeaky voice, with almost a whimper. Then she repeated the last sentence. "Mom, is Jeff gonna die?" She then bowed her head and let the tears drop off her face onto the front of her blouse.

I looked around to see everybody's reactions, saving myself from showing my own emotion. Corrinne's head was bowed down also, but without any tears. Her mom was staring at the wall in a trance. T.J. held a look of disbelief, like he still didn't want to accept the fact that one of our gang members was facing death. And Kristie was sitting on the couch, also with tears flowing down her cheek, but wiping away every trail that it had left, and putting out her lower lip, expressing her feelings with a pout. I sat there, in horror. But just sat there. It was one of those moments again, those reserved for theatrical drama. One that you would expect to happen to somebody else, and then say, "I hope I never have to deal with that." It was one of those moments that we were all dealing with. One that I thought I would never have to experience.

Chapter Eight

I finally came out of my trance. I was startled that I was in my college dorm room rather than in the hospital with Jeff. I looked to my left to see that Heather was no longer on my bed. I looked at the clock and realized that I had just wasted an hour of my life thinking about the past. The so-called experts in life say not to dwell on the past and I could understand why. Time in life is so short as it is, and dwelling on the past only makes it shorter.

I stood up and stretched my arms to the sky while yawning the practical yawn that everybody does when coming out of a daydream. I grabbed another beer out of the fridge and ripped off the top, which pretty much tore the skin off of my index finger. "Shit!" It was the only thing to say to myself. I grabbed a Kleenex and wrapped it around my finger and then held it there by a piece of scotch tape. It was almost eight o'clock at night, and suddenly Heather came prancing into my room and threw herself onto my bed. Frustrated that she had disturbed my solitude, I violently slapped her on the ass with a flicking motion to make it more painful, so that she would move.

"Ouch Doug!" She turned toward me with a disgusted look. "Did I say you could touch my ass?"

"Did I say that I wanted to? I'd do anything to get your ass out of my bed. Jus Ki. Jus Ki."

"Funny Doug. I'll tell you what I'm gonna do. I'm going to go get some food and when I get back, if you're not sleeping yet, you and I are going to do something."

"Wonderful," I thought to myself. She left the room and closed the door behind her lightly. "Shit!" This time I spoke it a little bit louder; yet quiet enough so that Heather wouldn't hear me just in case she was still outside the door. "I better get to sleep before she comes back." I kept talking to myself for some reason. Probably the fact that I had just come out of my daydream trance and didn't know anything that was going on.

I jumped on my bed and reached down to set the alarm on my clock for the next day, just in case I slept through the night. I set it for eight o'clock, even though I had an eight-fifteen class. After all, I could sleep in class, so there was no need to get all dressed up for naptime. My mind was clear and my body felt peaceful. I was far too comfortable for being in a college dorm. It was difficult for me to feel relaxed lately. I last remember zoning into thoughts of Jeff. Nothing in particular about him . . . just of him.

Chapter Nine

I woke up quickly, like I'd heard a bomb and was waking up to find shelter from an air raid. Once I awoke, I sat up and stared around the dark room for a while. I could barely see anything. Just the moonlight shining through our shades, making little silhouette shadows onto my dirty clothes, which lay on the floor. My roommate was snoring loudly. It sounded like a jet was flying through the room every time he would breathe in. Then when he would breathe out, it sounded like a ball of phlegm was stuck in his throat and that he was making a last ditch effort to get it out. Then a slight crackling sound would follow, as his throat struggled to escape the phlegm, and seemed to succeed for the moment, at least until the next breath of air.

I sat there thinking about the dream I had. It was a dream about my buddy. He was talking to me in the dream. His speech was a little slurred, a muffling sound came from behind his voice, but he was still up and about, walking around. I was working at some theme park and he just jumped over the counter and started talking to me. I was quite surprised and spoke as if I was. "Jeff, aren't you still supposed to be in the hospital . . . I-I-I mean, aren't you still hurt . . ." And then he spoke words to me which I don't think I could forget, and wouldn't ever want to.

"I whass . . . yeahh," still in that slurred, muffled voice of his. "Bud, I juss-t wunted ta tell you tat I wood be awright. I wiy-ull, I reawy wi-ull." He then hopped back over the counter, and walked away. I stared at him as he walked with that skinny body, looking like his upper body would fall off his legs, yet always failing to do so. My dream ended then, and that is where I woke up.

My hands were folded in prayer formation across my lap, even though I wasn't praying. I was stuck in that trance again, unable to move. I was in that state of mind where one wants to hope, yet afraid to do so in case that hope never becomes reality. One question kept running across my mind. Did this dream really mean that my buddy would be all right, or was it just a dream that makes me hope? I wondered if I would ever know. I mean, how much do dreams really mean?

I've had dreams before, or perhaps I should call them nightmares. Those nightmares where people die, or get seriously injured. I would wake up in a cold sweat just praying to God that no such horror would occur—and it usually didn't. So if no such horror usually occurred after a nightmare, then maybe nothing good would come out of this dream, either.

Of course, then again, I could look at what my sister told me. My sister and I went to the same college. She and I were really close. We always got along with each other, even as children, and would basically tell each other everything. She's one of the few people that I trust and respect. She's just a whole person all around—a little angel to me. She's always there for me when I have a problem, and even if I don't have a problem, she'll take me out to a bar and guarantee that I have a good time.

But what she told me scared the hell out of me. I visited her while she was at work one day, filtering through papers and placing the tabulated folders in the correct file cabinets. I walked around the desk and gave her a big smile—one of those bright smiles that I give when I'm happy to see someone, and I'm always happy to see her.

"Hey sis . . . how's it feel to have to work on such a day?" It was a sunny day, one of the few sunny days we'd get in the blistering cold winter months at Brockport.

"Well you know, I gotta pay the alcohol tab somehow. Yo—"

"I know exactly what you mean. I'm so low on money . . . The sad thing is that I'm more worried about not having enough money for alcohol this weekend than I am for other expenses. I mean, my phone bill run—"

"Doug . . ." She put her hands up in the air, indicating for me to hold on. "I hope you're not trying to tell me that a freakin' phone bill is more important than alcohol . . . C'mon."

All I could do was snicker. She always made me laugh. Especially with her alcohol jokes. "You know, I think you're right." A big grin made its appearance. "It's almost sad to say it, but that's the archetype of a college student."

I was in a good mood. It was rare for me to be in a good mood during a weekday. Usually I would go through the whole week depressed 'cause I had to do school work—until Thursday when I started drinking. That would cheer me up, the thought of going out to the bars and meeting women. But it wasn't a Thursday; it was still a Wednesday, yet I was in a good mood. That is, until my sister told me something that worried me.

"Doug . . . before you leave, I was meaning to talk to you about something." There was a short, silent pause.

"We . . . well, wh-what's that sis? Is it something about Jeff?" I just figured it was. I could tell by her drooping face, the quickly changing happy-to-sad expression that she availed.

"Well yeah. I mean, I don't know if his mom really wants anybody to know this . . . but I can trust you not to tell anybody, right?" A quick nod, almost like an automatic twitch, came from my head. "Well Jeff . . . h—"

"Is he alright?" The suspense was killing me. I had to find out immediately whether my buddy was o.k. or not.

"He's where he was at before. No changes yet. But look, can I just tell this story?" She waited there momentarily. She was probably waiting for an answer, but I couldn't say anything. My mind wanted to hear what she had to say about my buddy, and could not focus on anything else. So she went on.

"Jeff had these dreams a couple weeks before the accident an—"

"Can we please not call it an accident?" My voice was a little angry and uptight. She probably thought that I was mad at her, but I was just testy to the whole subject. I especially hated to hear it being called an accident, because accidents can be avoided. And I didn't want to think that my buddy was comatose in vain.

"O.K . . . anyway . . . he had these dreams a couple weeks before the-the . . . you know . . . and he would wake up in a cold sweat, just screaming for his mother. His mom would come to his side and ask him what was wrong . . . and he would explain to her that he had a dream about getting in a car acci- . . . sorry . . . in a car crash. And he was scared that it was really going to happen. She told him it was just a dream and it didn't mean anything, but then he had more of them. And each time he had this dream, he would wake up in a cold sweat and call for her. And each time she would tell him that it was just a dream, and that it didn't mean anything. But then you look at it now, and it kind of makes ya think, maybe dreams really can predict the future . . ."

There was a long moment of silence. An eerie feeling shot through my veins and sent a chill running from the bottom of my spine, sending the cold message up through my back until it hit the top of my neck, throwing my body into an uncontrollable seizure while I tried to gain stability. I felt like I was in a horror movie and this was when I was supposed to turn around to see the dreaded monster with a knife in hand and his arm stretched up, ready to strike. But I didn't look behind me. I just stood there, a couple sweat droplets forming on my nose, flowing to the cliff of it, yet hanging on for dear life—scared to fall to certain death, to certain fate.

I did finally manage to get some words out, although they sounded like words from a man with bronchitis—that sort of phlegm and hoarse throat sound.

"Di . . . Did he . . ." I let out a gasping cough hoping to clear my throat so that I could talk. "Did he die in the end of the dream?"

My sister once again acted surprised. "Well, I hope not . . . I mean, I'm not really sure how the dream ended. I didn't really ask his mom any questions." She then stared at the file cabinet for a moment, stared at nothing but the gray drawer, and began working again.

I walked out of that building and into the hazy world outside, allowing the fog to make its way around my body. I wondered then if maybe life was just a dream. Everything seemed so out of touch with reality. Or maybe I just forced myself to lose touch with reality so that the whole idea of a car crash wouldn't hurt so much.

It scared me so much, though. First of all, I'm a very strong believer in fate. I never used to believe in fate when I was in high school, but fate has shown some truth. And now that I was such a strong believer in the word, it scared me crazy to realize that his dreams actually did have some meaning to them.

I wasn't sure that I wanted to know how they ended. On this earth, one's fate is chosen, then fate looks for that person, and doesn't quit until it finds them. The worst part about it is that there's no stopping it. We just have to walk around life, as if nothing has or ever will go wrong—even though we know it has, and even though we know it will. So no, I didn't want to know the finale of his dreams. I would rather just keep a glimmer of hope and just walk around like everyone else, pretending that nothing ever bothers them. We humans need hope. Without it, there would probably be no reason for every person's aspirations and dreams. It's what keeps us going in everyday life and it's what helps us walk around like every one of those normal idiots. I call them idiots because they act oblivious to what's going on in their lives. But in order to function normally, you kind of have to be oblivious, or at least somewhat numb.

I thought about this as I continued to walk through my hazy

world. I looked down to my feet and watched each step I took. The fog surrounded me, and disconnected my feet from the rest of my body. It helped me feel numb to everything. My body lost all tenseness and my mind was cleared. I continued to walk in this new white world for as long as possible, but slowly the fog around me turned black, and then the silhouette shadows appeared, and reality struck me, pulling me out of my hazy world and back into my dorm room.

I plopped down onto my bed in my nightmarish life, with a misunderstanding of what reality even was. I didn't know what moment in time, what area, or even where I really was. For all I knew, I could've been the one in the coma. Maybe I was the one who was dreaming out my life and believing it was real, rather than living it.

Chapter Ten

Nothing in the world seemed like it was normal anymore. Every trip I made to see my buddy Jeff became more of a challenge. But it was a challenge that his parents had to deal with everyday, and so I would deal with it as much as I had to. In some way, maybe it could help to relieve the suffering of his family. But relieving their suffering seemed a near impossible task. When I first walked into the hospital room with my sister, I noticed the distraught face of his mother Kathy. She turned around and gave a slight grin, followed by a 'Hi', and then turned the other way to stare into Jeff's eyes. Gary, on the other hand, seemed more upbeat, although I'm sure he was hurting just as much on the inside. Many times when a husband is feeling hurt, he will grin and bear it as much as possible so that he can bring some life to the family, and with life, there is always hope.

"Hey, Jeff. How's the Spotter doin'?" I spoke as I walked closer to him and found a comfortable place on the side of his bed.

"He's been doing better lately." I could hear Mr. Nichols speaking to my sister behind me. "He appears to have some sort of idea of what's going on. We have a keyboard here, and we try and get him to play some music for us. He likes the music from that movie *Amadeus*. Steve came here and played it for him when he got home from college, and he seemed to smile when he played that for him."

I thought of the first time after Jeff got hurt that he gave me a slight smile. It was about a month after his car crash and I remember coming from Brockport College to see him. I walked in the hospital room and I recall his parents telling me that if I brought up something funny from the past, then he might smile a little. So I started making fun of the spot on his cheek and calling him names. I basically just brought up times of the past that we shared together. And it was when I brought up the time we spent at Kistner Concrete together that he let loose with a little smile. It was hard to tell if he smiled for sure because of the neural damage that had been done. But it looked enough like one to me to realize that he remembered the good times of the past. At least some of them. That made me realize that the old Jeff was still in there, struggling to get out of his helpless situation. Jeff and I had once wanted to help Damian escape the Kistner Concrete workers, but could do nothing because we were helpless ourselves. And now, though everybody tried hard to help Jeff, nobody could do anything for the same reason—we were all helpless ourselves. It was up to Jeff to help himself, if he could.

I wondered how Jeff could remember the good times of the past, even after his traumatic situation. But I realized, it's no wonder those memories remained unscathed in his brain. After all, the time after our near faltering mission with the Kistner Concrete workers, I began to wallow in deep thoughts about the bond between friends. In my immature and therefore, inept wisdom, I could hardly understand the significance of where those beginning thoughts were to lead. But through my increased age and experience, and my wisdom gained through Jeff's car crash, I came to more of an understanding of the friendship bond.

It is probably one of the most important, and also one of the most difficult to break. And when you think about it, it's no wonder we are able to form this type of relationship with somebody. This earth began in that way and continues to progress in this nature. It's like the chemical bond between atoms, or the attraction of one element to another. It's the sodium atom that will bond with the chlorine atom because it has seven electrons in its valence shell. Since the sodium atom has one electron in its valence shell, it will join with the chlorine to receive fulfillment. This is like the friends who join with each other, because they know they can bond with each other, and they need each other to fulfill one another's lives. It is these elements which make up the earth, and which control the movements and actions in humans' everyday lives. So it is no wonder that we are like the atom, needing a bond to satisfy our very existence. And Jeff's memories must've remained, because good memories between friends with an invigorated bond are most difficult to break—even by some brute physical force.

The thoughts ran through my head until I felt the touch of a keyboard on my hand. I snapped my head back in wonder of what to do with it.

Gary spoke his words softly, assuring me that I was doing something worthwhile. "Would you like to play something for him on the keyboard? He might like it."

I grabbed the keyboard for lack of something to say to Jeff, and I began playing a song which he had taught me, "Let It Be." Jeff had taught me that song one day when we had gotten back from taking some of his grandmother's cans back to the store.

The song probably relaxed him, especially since his mother sang along with it. She had a very beautiful voice. Everywhere you look in the Nichols' family, they're so full of talent. Some of it hidden, and some of it showing in all its glory. Jeff had some amazing talents himself, especially in athletics. But it could only be left to the imagination as to how many hidden talents he had. I struggle every time I think of how he might never be able to walk or talk again, or to express his feelings, or to become the success that he could've been. He was a true leader at heart, but he never had the chance to prove it. Jeff was a kid with very intricate thoughts and emotions, so full of zeal and motivation, but rarely revealing his feelings and aspirations. He was a walking four-leaf clover, full of good luck and seemingly magical abilities. He was the face on my 1977 Abe Lincoln penny, which I had always used during poker games. The only difference between Jeff and that great American hero Abe Lincoln is that the past President stayed healthy enough to conquer his dreams and aspirations. Jeff was injured far before his prime. I get so angry when I think of all the talent that could've shone through, had the mishap not occurred.

I broke my train of thought purposely and started playing rap tunes for him on the keyboard. I told a story to his parents so they would understand why I was always playing rap tunes around Jeff. "One time we made a song about T.J. and the whole song was about his snout. We completely tore him apart in the song and then rapped it to T.J. when we next saw him. And I also figured since Jeff was so into Snoop Doggy Dogg, that he likes to hear little tunes every now and then." His mom just smiled, realizing the craziness in all our little adolescent games. So I went on with the drumbeat, half rap tune playing on the keyboard.

"I sing a little rap for my main man Spot, 'cause walkin' with the E.B. gang and a girlie that's hot. Playin' his game of basketball, struttin' it nice like he's got it all." Then I stopped for lack of better words. Jeff seemed to enjoy it because he had that kind of sparkly look in his eyes. He couldn't talk or anything but it seemed as if he knew what was going on around him, at least to a certain extent. Every time we would come to the hospital, there were always small improvements.

I started another rap tune and grabbed his hand to make him do the famous rap-like movement. The hand in the air, flat, and sort of jiving to the beat type of movement. "Jeff and Doug were walkin' 'long the street, lookin' for some ladies, gettin' hot with the heat, drivin' 'long in a new Mercedes . . ." I went along for a little while, thinking of the experiences that we shared together, Jeff and I. It seemed like we were almost back in the old times again. Like things were the way they used to be. The times we would spend together shooting pop bottles full of water with his shotgun, or playing around in a duck pond near his house on a little blow-up raft. Or things like going to his house after school, before baseball practice and just shooting around the basketball with all our trash talking and 'yo mama' jokes that we used to do. It was little things like that which I sometimes missed the most. And it was one of those little things I was doing. And for a small moment, it seemed like things were getting back to normal and maybe there was a hope that someday, Jeff would also be normal.

But as we said our good-byes to the family and were on our way out of the hospital to make our way back to Brockport, I looked back at Jeff. He was lying down in bed with his mother by his side clutching his hand, tears nearly running down her face. Gary stood by Kathy's side, rubbing her shoulders and giving her loving kisses on the neck for reassurance. There was hope inside them, and there was hope inside myself. That's what made it hurt all the more. The fact that everybody had so much hope and the realization of what might never happen.

I had meant to tell the Nichols family something, although I was sure they already knew. I even had a newspaper clipping in my wallet to remind myself. It was an article titled, *Glory Is Of The Heart*. It was an article about the Pavilion High School basketball team and their championship run. Pavilion was the small farm school where we all used to go, where Jeff would still be, and the basketball team made it to the finals. They lost in the finals, but the important thing about the article is that Jeff was the main focus of it.

A nurse from the hospital had brought Jeff to the game hoping to expose him to familiar surroundings and external stimuli, and pull him more out of his coma. The picture, which was featured on the front page, was of a basketball teammate and friend in school, hugging Jeff while tears ran down his face. The grimace on his face showed the pain that he was feeling ... the pain that we were all feeling. And there was Jeff, his eyes nearly shut, his mouth open and his head cocked back onto his wheelchair in a sleeping position. His snow colored white hat seemed to fit perfectly onto his head in the picture, but in reality the hat was loose to protect the soft indent on his head.

This was Jeff's spotlight. Sitting in a chair unable to watch what his destiny should have been. Except, he would've changed the outcome of the game. He would have made happen what was meant to happen. Fate must have made a mistake somewhere along the line, because it took the wrong kid. He would've cashed that three pointer; I just know he would have. I know it because I've seen him do it a thousand times, if not more. I saw it my senior year when I played basketball with him on the team. I saw it every time when my friends and I would play at his house. Make after make after make of the three pointer, and only missing when it didn't really matter, but always making it when the pressure was on.

The team could've used that three pointer then. It would've saved them from losing. It would've brought the basketball championship home to a school that hasn't won it in over thirty years. It would have boosted him into a college of his choice, and onto an intercollegiate team of his choice. It would've given him the spotlight . . . a real spotlight. One that could be enjoyed by himself as well as by his fans. I could just see the game in my head, the way the game should've been. And I could hear myself chanting the play-by-play. The play-by-play the way it should've been said.

"Jeff Nichols has the ball with ten seconds to play and he is dribbling down the court. He dribbles past two men and has only one to beat before he reaches his half of the court. Whoa, he burnt that guy. Do I smell toast? Only three seconds to play, this is pressure. Jeff Nichols stops at the three-point line. He stopped dead there and is shooting up a three pointer!" And the lights from the cameras would be flashing. And the fans in the crowd would be at a standstill in time, holding their breaths to see the outcome of his shot. A fat lady sitting by herself because she takes up three seats on the Pavilion side, would stop eating her nachos with extra, extra, extra cheese for one second to see the shot. And Jeff would be watching, standing there in his strange shooting posture, with a sparkle in his eye. He would release the ball with the confidence of a professional, and he'd be staring with a big smile on his face, his eye's casting stardom gloriously, and his skinny arms raised in the air ready to swing in a boxer's motion to cheer on his game winning shot. Then the ball would flutter above the basket, ready to make its entrance into the net, and the beautiful swoosh sound ready to make its outburst. And then . . . and then my imagination stopped and I snapped out of what I was thinking. I allowed realization to conquer my spirit. Jeff wasn't in that game because fate wouldn't let him be. The net—which wanted to hold its little baby in its womb forever— never could. The roaring cheers never did come. That net never did allow the ball to pass through to achieve its fate . . . because Jeff wasn't there to make that game winning shot. Jeff could not achieve one of his dreams. Fate wouldn't allow him to.

It's weird because Jeff taught me that song "Let It Be." Sometimes I think Jeff had more reasoning than life itself. Here this kid was, teaching me a song to just let things be, to just let them happen. And yet, life wouldn't just let him be, it wouldn't just let him happen. Life had to send out its little hitman called fate. And it had to track Jeff down right before the prime of his life. The senior year of high school. The year where you make all your plans of success for the future, yet enjoy every moment of the present, and no longer give a shit about anything that has happened in your past.

Fate is a strange component of life in itself. Not everybody believes in fate. Some believe that life is planned out for us humans while some believe that we make things happen. I do believe in fate. But I also believe that you can make things happen . . . just as long as fate doesn't get in the way. But I admit that sometimes I wonder if our life is planned out for us. Maybe everything we do is out of our control. Maybe the serial killer that kills because he likes to, has no control over what he's doing. Sometimes I feel like everything is interconnected in some way. That every aspect of our lives leads up to some event that is going to happen in the future. That every dust particle, every piece of dirt, and every imprint that is made in that dirt by our worn out shoes . . . has meaning. Maybe those people I talked about, those that throw their potential away into a life of drugs and alcohol—into a black hole of nothingness—do so because that is their fate and they were meant to end up that way.

I remember the time Jeff took us to McDonald's in his old red truck. T.J. had said, 'You better hope you don't ever get in an accident with this piece . . . you'll have no chance for survival.' And then Jeff, with his cocky, yet sly reply. 'You wouldn't have any chance for survival . . . but when you're built like me, you have no worries. Jus Ki, Jus Ki.'

And then how we almost hit the 18-wheeler truck. I would normally throw it off as coincidental, but I can't get past the chill I felt while talking to Jeff at McDonald's. That seeming presence from the future warning me, or guiding me to some thought or idea. The fact that the feeling came directly after we had almost gotten killed in a car crash is nearly inconceivable. It makes me think now . . . possibly life was just warning me that it had sent out its little hitman, and was on its way to take control of Jeff's life. All this possibility of what life really is, sending everybody into mass confusion on what to do in a situation like Jeff's. Sometimes I prefer not to think about anything at all, and just watch life go by. And at the same time, I want to live life, before fate takes control of me and puts me in the same situation as Jeff.

I think of the times when my friends and I used to go to Kistner Concrete and harass the construction workers. I think of the feeling I had after our successful missions, that everlasting happiness. I thought nothing could ruin that feeling. I thought the rest of my life was made just for fun. But I was wrong, because now I wonder if I'll ever get that feeling of happiness back. I used to think that 'Time heals all wounds'. I was wrong again. Now I wonder if the part of my heart that Jeff was in will ever heal with anything but scar tissue, enough so that I don't remember the pain everyday of my life. I try to deny my pain, but it's down there, just eating away at me and feasting on my insides like a microscopic parasite. It's microscopic because I can't see it, I can only feel it. And there's no cure for it. Then I think of the pain that Jeff has to go through everyday of his life. I hope there's a heaven, because Jeff will be there someday. Of that, I have no doubt in my mind. If there's not, then I feel sorry that he has to miss out on all that's good in life.

My feeling of everlasting happiness is destroyed, and if Jeff can even feel, then his is also. And every person who knew Jeff, or who knew somebody else who had been acquainted with Jeff, also has a tainted happiness. Nothing lasts forever on this earth. Nothing except for the pain. That aching feeling in my heart every time I look at that picture. The breaking of my heart in two every time I think of what might have been. And a deep sadness in those broken pieces every time I think of what can never be.

I folded up the picture and placed it back into my leather wallet. I put it behind my driver's license. Now every time that I drive, every time that I pull out my license to show a policeman . . . I will remember him. And I will realize that I need to be cautious so that fate doesn't take me. I love and hate fate all at the same time. It can make you into a star or it can turn you into a vegetable. So now I just sit back and see what it wants to make of me.

Chapter Eleven

The freshman year of college was finally coming to a close. It certainly wasn't the ideal year, but it wasn't the worst either. Of course, I thought of Jeff everyday. And I had some scares at college. The average 'poor grade performance' scare and getting into drunken fights, all those fun things that our warped American society loves to experience.

I was packing my stuff together and bringing it down to my car before I had to pick up my sister. Being practically the last one out of the dorm, I had to make a few trips up two flights of stairs with hundreds of pounds worth of luggage and worthless materials in my hands. Most of what seemed to fill up my suitcases, sadly enough, were the pitchers and cups that I stole in my drunken moments from the bars. Don't get me wrong; I'm not a big time kleptomaniac. I just needed some souvenirs from my favorite hangouts. After all, I had been planning to take the next year off to join the Army National Guard and mull over what I wanted to do in life, because I had no idea where my life was headed. I took down all the pictures from my desk bulletin board and tossed the worn out tacks into the garbage. I looked for a moment at the picture, one of the few things besides my sister, dog, and beer that still made me happy in life. The picture of the three most famed members of the E.B. gang standing together at my high school graduation party, arms around each other and smiles on our faces, staring at the camera in our half-cocked formation. I smiled and nodded, whispering to myself, "Oh, the good ol' days." I taped it carefully to a quote that was once on my door: "It ain't over til' it's over." It's a quote from baseball phenom, Yogi Berra. After his playing years, when he managed the New York Mets, he said that significant statement when his team was nine games out of first place in the National League. That same year, that same team came back to gain first place status and win the pennant.

I was in a slight hurry. I had to pick up my sister, get back home, talk with the family, and still have time to get to a friend's house for a welcoming home party. After I got to her dorm with a greeting of, "We have to hurry, beers awaiting us," we found ourselves on the half-hour trip back home to relief from stress.

My mother was happy to see us at the door and my dog was twice as happy. It was soothing to feel his slobbery licks all over my face, even if it does sound disgusting. A kiss from a loyal dog to me is just as good as a kiss from the girl you love, although that's as far as I'd go with that saying. The rest is better to do with a girlfriend, unless you're more on the alternative lifestyle side. It was relaxing to be home again. The warmth of being back home is probably the best feeling that could ever be experienced in one's lifetime. After talking for a while and eating supper, I readied myself for the party across the street. I was already late because the party started at midday, with everybody trying to get their drinking fill in before the keg was empty.

Once I got there, the first words I heard from the partygoers was, "Time for another beer run." My kind of party I thought. I saw Steve over on the trampoline, trying to do a complete flip in the air, but many times landing on his ass or head. "Steve, compadre!" I screamed out to him but he didn't hear me in his concentrating state of mind. I screamed much louder. "Steve, compadre, I'm talking to you!" Still not hearing me, I decided to take matters into my own hands and shot toward him at a full-fledged sprint and tackled him onto the trampoline, causing us both to bounce up as high as the roof and land flat faced on the grass.

"You asshole, what did you do that for?" Steve said it in his trying-to-be-mad tone, but gave away his seriousness with a smirk.

"Sorry man, I just had to greet you with the ol' East Bethany tackle."

"Well, I'm from Pavilion. And I also have a career to think about. A successful man like me has to be careful of such injuries to avoid trauma that may affect my stability in the future."

Kristie let out a, "Oh Steve, relax. Cocky guys like you don't deserve success so accept the tackle as a loving gesture to bring you down to earth."

Of course, Steve always having a comment for everything, came out with another snide remark. "Cocky guys like me is what keeps the success of America in the Nichols' genes."

"Please Steve, it's a good thing they're going on another beer run. I think you need to drink a little more to bring you back to reality."

I couldn't handle the trash talking between him and my sister right then. I needed to drink. I waited for about ten minutes by the door so that I would get the best selection of beer, and was gratefully welcomed with the opening of the door and a full keg being brought in. I went up to pat the two struggling men on the shoulders and noticed that one of them was Jay, the driver of the car in Jeff's tragedy. I stopped dead in my tracks and dropped my cup as they walked past. Jay didn't look any too happy. He dropped the keg in its position and made a trip to the kitchen table, where he sat down and began guzzling his warm beer left over from before he went. I stood across the kitchen until my sister and Steve finally walked in and screamed at me to grab a beer. I snapped out of my trance and grabbed my cup off the counter to fill it up. I filled Steve another cup and handed it to him. He took it from me, but without a sound and without a nod of gratitude.

"Hey, a simple thank you would be appropriate." But no word or nod yet came. I looked into his eyes and followed his gaze to see where his sight was directed. I found his eyes blazed on Jay, with no expression of emotion.

Jay looked up and saw Steve, his old time track buddy. They met eye to eye for no more than a split second. Jay changed sights and looked down at his feet, stood up with his head still hanging down and left the room, without notice by the other partiers. Steve continued to stare at what was now a ghostly figure in the chair. I walked into the next room and could barely stand the memories of sadness, which continued to linger in everybody's mind. It was, in essence, the time when I feared getting caught by the Kistner Concrete workers. The moment I sat in between the prickly trees with Jeff, and said—'Dude man . . . I gotta admit, I'm kinda scared. If any of us get caught, we're all goin' down.' And everybody 'goin down', in a sense, is exactly what had happened. It captured the whole town of Pavilion where Jeff lived, and every town next to it where all his friends were affected. I did the only thing I felt I could do. I sat down on the couch and drank beer after beer, only getting up for a refill to swig down another.

I heard people calling for Jay—which echoed throughout a house, which now seemed more like a prison. Kristie to my relief, walked into the room about a half-hour later to let me know they were leaving and ask if I wanted to come.

"Yeah." It was all I could squeak out. I went home, put on a sleeveless shirt, and got in bed. I slept until the next afternoon, where I was rudely awakened by another dream of the past times we shared together. I woke up realizing that I would have to spend another day of life with the memories on my mind. A snarl shook forth from my lips and a groaning from beneath my chest; crazy thoughts ran through my mind, telling me not to feel—that I couldn't feel because it was too painful, a pain that I had been trying to hold back since the car crash happened in October. A day that would live in infamy and an anniversary which would preferably never make its passing each year. I was ready to break out in a blood rush of anger when a ring of the phone broke my rage into tiny spurts of anxiousness. I picked up the phone after the first ring with a quick, "Hello, who art thou?"

"Doug man, what the hell's with the Shakespeare act?"

"T.J., my brother, it's good to hear from you. My Shakespearean act comes from the fact that I'm sober enough to think."

"Well, that's something new coming from my E.B. brother. Where were you last night? I tried to give you a call."

I let out a sigh of distemper with the fact that he brought up the quite forgettable welcoming home party I had. He was probably curious why I had gotten so frustrated with his simple question so I answered quickly to avoid a follow-up remark on his part. "Oh, I was at a friend's welcoming home party. I called you but your papa said you were at some girl's house getting laid."

"He told you I was getting laid?" T.J. broke out in a question of disbelief that his father might have known what his son had been doing in his spare time.

"I'm just kidding my man. He just said you were at some girl's house." I couldn't help but laugh at my funny comment to scare my best friend, and it helped take my mind off of things for the time being, so I was in a much better mood. "Look man, why don't we drink tonight before we start our jobs that we don't yet have."

I was supposed to be working full-time at $6.50 an hour with some guy that my mother knew. He would have brought me into work so that I could save on gas, and he also would have been my boss at work. The job didn't work out though, because the business closed down, so the bad luck just continued for me. I figured I might as well enjoy the time I had off and party as much as possible, there was nothing else to do in East Bethany.

"Yeah, no problem. I just have to help my dad with some lawnmower stuff around here. I'll be over around seven o'clock tonight. Then we'll go pick up some brew and start drinking."

I waited around throughout the day, shot some hoops by myself and sat inside watching my favorite movie called *Braveheart*. It was a movie about a Scottish warrior who fought for what he believed in, which was freedom. I like stories where people believe in what they're doing. I figure that's what life's all about, believing in something. If you don't have anything to believe in, then you may as well die, because there's not much else to live for.

I last remember watching the part where the Scottish warrior was talking with this gorgeous princess inside his prison cell. She was an English princess, yet she loved this Scottish warrior. She was begging for him to take a drug to numb his pain because she couldn't bare the thought of his torture and death. His reply was, "Every man dies, not every man really lives." Then I dozed off. I was awakened in the middle of one of my sexual dreams just when it was getting exciting. A beer bottle was being put in my mouth, which unfortunately turned my dream into a homosexual dream, which naturally woke me up.

"What the hell? I looked around myself with squinted eyes and saw T.J. with a big grin on his face. "Do you realize what you just woke me up from?"

"Nothing can be more important than beer, my man."

"Sex isn't more important than beer?"

"Oh, I'm sorry." He sounded so sincere. He must have realized that interfering in anything sexual, whether a dream or reality, is one of the more serious crimes to commit on an eighteen-year old male. "Dude, why didn't you tell me you were having one of those dreams?"

I stared at him, and that was all. It was the dumbest question that I had ever heard and I was hoping he would tell me he was kidding. But he sat down and began drinking his beer. I opened one for myself, without another word. We sat there and watched TV for about an hour and a half, and guzzled about eight beers in that time span, before T.J. finally spoke.

"You know what I've been thinking?"

I didn't feel compelled to say anything. I was feeling a pretty good buzz at that point and didn't want to say anything in fear that my buzz might be disturbed. So he went on.

"I've been thinking Crook . . . a lot actually . . . about Jeff."

I continued to stare at the TV. The name Jeff was in my everyday life. Whether somebody brought it up to me or not, I would always think about him.

"I think of things like how I've treated people. Like how I've treated my ex-girlfriend . . ." He paused for a moment, waiting for a reply to assure him that I heard what he was saying. I was becoming interested in what he had to say, so I turned my head, eyeing him with all intensity. "The way in which I used to cheat on her and not even tell her. And then I see Jeff . . . this innocent kid. Never hurt a soul. Never hurt a damn thing. He just lived and never gave a shit about what others had over him. He just lived and got punished for being good."

I sat there for a moment, sipped my beer, and then spoke. "Don't look at it that way. Look at it in the way that you were lucky. God allowed you to live, so make the best of it while you're here."

T.J. continued on. "I mean, when I got dicked around by that Wendy girl, now I realize that I deserved it." That cute, little blonde that T.J. had been dating didn't take too kindly to his want of a more serious relationship.

"T.J. man, don't be so har—"

"I deserved everything I got for the way I treated my ex-girlfriend. But what did Jeff do to deserve this?" He paused again, now without the realization or even the care of whether or not I was listening. "The boy got screwed over and now he can't even get cocked with us." He put the brew to his mouth and guzzled down the beer. But only to reach down for another, open the top and fire it into the box, and then chug down another. It took a matter of thirty seconds for him to finish the two beers. And he probably ended up finishing two more within the next five minutes.

I turned my head back toward the television and tried to be

strong. I watched some comedian spraying whipped cream out into his audience from some supposedly used condom. The crowd was laughing hysterically. I didn't find it too funny. In fact, I found it quite annoying. I began to squint my eyes, falling into a near relapse of sleep. Thoughts flowed through my head, exiting my brain just as quickly as they had entered. I couldn't hold one thought long enough to sort it out. I only knew that what T.J. had said was exactly what I had been thinking all along. That only the good ones suffer.

The comedian on the television put the condom on his head and around his chin so that there wasn't an opening where air could enter or escape. With the air that he had trapped in the condom, he sucked in through his mouth, and then exhaled through his nose so that the condom ballooned while still on top of his head, making his head look like a large condom in itself. The crowd was in absolute hysteria, while I had not even chuckled on the inside. Not even one of those inside laughs that you give people when they make a stupid joke and you don't want them to feel uncomfortable. They ask you, "How come you didn't laugh?" And you tell them, "I was laughing on the inside." My mind was still on Jeff.

I thought of the time, a week or two before he got in the car crash, when I told him, "You'll get yours Jeff . . . someday you'll receive the shock . . . and when you least expect it, too." That sentence painted itself in my mind. It was an everlasting bulletin, advertising to my conscious until I could no longer handle the guilt. I grabbed my last beer and snapped off the top with my bare hand, putting a cut in my thumb and causing blood to run down my wrist. I must have looked suicidal at that point, like I was trying to slice the major blood vessels in my wrist. Before I got any ideas, I took off my old torn up, sleeveless white shirt and wrapped my thumb in it. I fired the top at T.J., trying to wake him up in his drunken, passed-out stage. I needed someone to keep me company to take my mind off of everything. But he didn't wake up. So I grabbed my last hope by the neck and drained it into my throat like I had done so many times before, only allowing little droplets onto my outer lips, which I licked up once I had finished my beer. I controlled the beer's fate. For once, I was the one in a position of power. But to continue on as such, the beer could certainly begin controlling my fate.

The sentence continued to taunt me. "You'll get yours Jeff . . . someday you'll receive the shock . . . and when you least expect it, too." Over and over it continued, but changing slightly so that it began to flash through my mind like one of those broken billboards that continue to blink the same message. The ones that you can't stop because they are too high or too hard to fix. I stuck in a dip of Mint Skoal chewing tobacco, which I many times did when I wanted to relax. But my heart began beating faster; palpating itself louder with each flash of the message, and playing a drum beat to make a mockery of my guilt. I needed something to distract my ruminating mind. So I began whispering the obvious to myself. "You were only talking about the electric fence, Doug." I whispered it over and over until I was relaxed enough to think a little more clearly.

I heard the claps of the crowd on TV. I hadn't heard them laugh much in the last half of his performance. I don't know if it was because I wasn't really paying attention or because they finally realized how annoying the comedian was. The comedian walked off stage with the condom still on his head, but with a big hole in the nose area for him to breathe through. Then the screen faded to the color black and a loud beeping began. The beeping continued and visions of the phone conversation danced in front of me. I saw myself holding the phone, in a trance. The annoying beeping continuing, and my mind just wandering. I quickly grabbed the remote and shut off the TV, so the room was pitch dark. I did this to hold myself back from crying, and to save my image as somebody who would not feel the pain. I told myself, "Something good always comes out of something bad." I whispered it out to myself again so my ears could hear it and so my brain could understand it.

I began to think of good things that might possibly come out of Jeff's situation. I thought of how my sister and Steve were getting much closer together at the hospital. I thought of how it might bring them back together into a destiny that was meant for them, to be together for life or longer. Then crazy ideas began entering my mind. Things like how my injured buddy would drive me to do something great—something heroic or something helpful, so that Jeff wouldn't be comatose in vain. And maybe it wasn't so crazy. Every time I think of Jeff, I feel this yearning deep down inside me. This yearning to succeed. A little voice telling me not to ruin my life, that I have been lucky enough to remain alive. And to make something of that life and fulfill all those dreams which the other after-lifers would be sharing with so much enthusiasm. To make myself into something heroic or something helpful. 'Something good always comes out of something bad', I thought.

I walked into the kitchen in my drunken stupor and reached above the fridge to grab a notebook, losing my balance and causing a poem called 'Don't Quit' to fall to the floor. It was a poem my mom had used to help her quit smoking. It seems kind of like the wrong poem to use to quit something, but I guess she used it to mean, "don't quit on quitting", or something like that. I picked up the poem and set it on the table for lack of being able to find its magnet.

"I could write a poem, that sounds like fun." I said the words aloud since nobody could hear me anyway. I had originally planned to use the notebook to write to some friends at college, but seeing the poem on the table inspired me to do something creative.

I stumbled back to the couch and plopped myself down, more from being unable to stand rather than from wanting to sit. I had forgotten a pen while in the kitchen and unable to stand again, I reached down into the crevices of the couch and just prayed for a pen to be there. Luckily enough, I found a black pen with the cover all gnawed apart and the ink pouring out the back. I began writing with no direction whatsoever, and just wrote down whatever came to mind.

Why Won't My Buddy Get Up . . . I looked at the title, and chuckled to hold back my tears. And I began writing again.

> My Buddy lies there as the world lives on, in a coma
>   barely able to move his arm.
> More innocent than an angel, yet life has cast him tough-
>   ness.
> It seems almost unbearable to watch his family hope,
>   when deep down they feel a nothingness.
> No more poker, one-on-one basketball or playing base-
>   ball.
> No more home run derby, when we'd try our hardest to hit
>   the ball over the wall.
> The good times we had in his rusted up old red truck.
> The laughs we had over him calling me the nickname
>   Crook.
> I remember the last party this summer, when all my friends
>   were there.
> All the criticisms we had of each other, yet no one seemed
>   to care.
> Then he drove us to get some McDonald's fast food.
> We talked over old times, and he put us all in a good
>   mood.
> The last time I saw him was when I came home from
>   college.
> We went outside to test out his electric dog collar.
> It's quite ironic 'cause now I've had the shock of my life.
> My sports buddy is now dealing with a life of strife.
> Now only the unanswerable question is left
> And sometimes I even ask God, "Why won't my buddy
>   get up . . ."

I tore the sheet of paper out of the notebook. I did it slowly, as if I didn't have enough energy to do it faster. But I did have energy. I just didn't have any emotion left. My broken heart was hardening into stone, and my scattered mind was making its transformation into insanity. I shuddered to think of what the family was going through.

When I had finished ripping the page out of the notebook, I folded it into eleven creases, for his baseball number. Then I grabbed an empty beer bottle from my case of twelve. I pushed the poem down to the bottom. And there it would stay until my buddy came out of his coma, and until he could once again play sports and drink beers with us. I put the bottle firmly back into its place in the middle of all the rest of the beer bottles. The bottles were just like his life. He was in the middle of friends and very well liked by everybody, just as this bottle was in the middle of all the rest of his bottle buddies. But like the beer, Jeff got his life taken away. His insides were all taken out of him . . . his emotions, his love, his hate, and his ability to do anything that he wanted and desired. And now he sits, still amongst friends, family and loved ones, but all of whom have their insides taken out. Their emotions, their love, their hate, and the ability to live life the way it once was. Now all that is left is hope, probably a false hope. And a struggle to the top with expectations of a miracle prayed for by St. Jude and the possibility of an ongoing disappointment, but still with hope. And so the hunger continues.

I sat there with the light fading in and out, and my eyes gazing at the clock and nothing else. I was a minute human on the face of the treacherous earth and I was struggling with the best of them no matter how strong I tried to be. Holding back the tears became more of a struggle everyday that I woke, every night that I slept. I could feel the burning of salt running down my throat, struggling to escape through my eyes and wishing for some guiding light to lead them into the right direction. And finally, the tears began to come. All my attempts at holding them back turned out to be unsuccessful.

It started off with one tear, a fighter that led all the other tears to come forth and follow him. And they did. I cried like I did when I was twelve years old, and nothing I did could contain it. My pain was pouring forth with all its strength and my heart was beating slowly, with no more than a fading hope that it might once again be revived with the life it once held. The tears poured forth, into my mouth, down my cheeks, and making a slobbering mess of my eyes so the clock became more of a fixture on the wall rather than the passage of time. My sobbing became louder and my loneliness grew higher. T.J. was in the room, but I was alone. I was alone because I knew of no other way to feel. And my sobbing continued with a couple whispers of, "It's been so hard, it's been so hard. God, I don't know how much longer I can handle it. I just don't know." And then the crying stopped. It stopped like it had just been caught in the middle of a crime, so abruptly.

I stood up and went to my full-length mirror. It was dark, but a slight light from the moon which shined down upon the mirror gave me enough light to see. I noticed that my shirt was a wet mess and my face was the same. I couldn't decide which was wetter, my shirt or my face. But I soon came to the conclusion that my face was, so I used my shirt to wipe every tear off my face and out of my eyes, as well as every trail that it had left behind. Except one remained. The leader had made its way almost to my shirt and then stopped there before being soaked up by the cotton. It was still in watery formation, sitting there on my collarbone. I just left it there. I left it there because I didn't see the purpose in wiping it away. My bloodshot teary eyes just stared at that tear . . . that enemy which I was so tired of fighting.

I came back to the couch and once again plopped on top of it. My loveable dog Harley then came hobbling out from the hallway. He was putting on more weight with every day that came and went, but I love every part of him just as much; there's just more of him to love. He came up to me, and as I bent down to pet him; he gave me a lick directly on the nose. Then with his big, brown eyes he looked directly into mine, letting me know that he was there for me. And though it was a comfort to realize this, it was sad at the same time. Not for me, but for the Nichols' family. I could understand how important it is to be able to love one who loves you, as I did with my dog. But for the Nichols' family, though there was still an open love for one another, the ability to show and act on such a relationship would never be the same because Jeff would never be the same.

It then occurred to me—the way life works, or at least, cause no one will ever know, a possibility to the way life works. Suddenly all the events of the past came streaming into my mind into a large whirlwind of an idea. It occurred to me that everything in life is connected. Those sweat droplets which hang on for dear life as they flow to the cliff of my nose, or the sweat which struggled through my brow, or the tears which left a burning of salt in my throat because they were looking for some guiding light to help them escape through my eyes, and me struggling to hold back those tears. Or how about the air which struggled to move out of the way of the basketball after Jeff's shot, and the ball which struggled with hope to stay away from the ground—even though it knew it would continue to hit the ground and repeatedly meet its fate. And now Jeff struggles to get out of his helpless situation.

I then realized: everything in life is connected in a struggle to fight through pain—caused by fate, fought through with hope. Yet we struggle because we have hope, and because we struggle, there is more pain. But we humans need hope ... to fulfill our dreams that we so heartily believe in, to move on and fight the destruction which fate can produce.

It's a vicious circle in life, the way we humans think and feel. But after all, the universe is just one big circle—as the universe is always repeating its course of action. The round moon, which rotates around the round earth. And the round earth, which rotates around the round sun. The universe which moves around in this vicious circle possibly is why humans think, act, and live their daily lives in this vicious circle—always repeating our past and being controlled by fate, which comes around to control our actions again and again.

It is logical to say that everything that makes a human up is what a human is. The atoms that bind our bodies together into one big multi-molecular structure called a human, also binds us through gaseous molecules to one another. And we are not only bound in science, but in soul. The sweat that struggles through the brow or the tear that struggles to escape the eye are part of ourselves. With sweat and tears we struggle to fight through pain— caused by fate, fought through with hope.

Hope . . . a word that never seems to get you anywhere, but never fails to bring you somewhere. I now hope that I can move on into the future, though I know the universe won't let me move on completely. The past, which I tried to leave behind once before when I left for college, was brought back to me. Now I know that a past cannot be forgotten, but also must not be dwelled upon. Rather, it should be held in fond memory.

I thought of many times my friends and I shared together, about times we had at Kistner Concrete. Most of the workers we used to harass no longer worked there, finding a new job with more pay. I don't know if there was a new bunch of E.B. boys, but if there was, they will never pull off some of the stunts that we did. The Huffy bike that Damian had once used for transportation had the wheels all torn off by some neighborhood kids, and the bike itself is rusting into the gravel that it lies on. The SNK baseball game that Jeff had worked so hard to build up a baseball team on was broken, with all the teams on it erased from the computer memory. Now if I could only erase the horrible memory that taunted me, the thought of the car crash. And Jay Vandermeer, the driver of the car in the crash, had quit cross-country and moved to a different school to play football. It's no doubt because the memories of Jeff were etched too far into his mind, causing him only pain every time he ran.

The E.B. Gang itself would also—over time—vanish into the earth as if it had never existed in the first place. Damian would end up going to grad school as an English major, while travelling the U.S. every summer with the little money he got from a couple months worth of full-time work. A couple of more friends would end up dying in a car crash—sliding on ice and barreling into an 18-wheeler truck. John Suozzi would then move to North Carolina to live with his mother. Imaginably, because the loss of too many friends is too much for the human soul to bear. And T.J. would fall in love with a new girl—and spend the majority of his little spare time with her.

I reached to my left to turn on an Atlanta Braves lantern, which was on top of the boxes that I still hadn't unpacked. Seeing the lantern made me think of baseball. It brought me back to one time in particular when I was a senior in high school. I remember it so clearly. I held the lantern up to my face to make my imagination more realistic, and pretended the lantern was the hot sun bearing down on me that day. My mind wandered and I could almost see the screen of my imagination getting blurry, taking me away from reality once again and allowing me to live in my past, the good part of my past, for just a moment.

The sun was very hot that day and my buddies were kidding around with me on the bench. "You stupid asshole, why the hell would you wear a turtleneck on a day like this?"

"Hey, he probably wants to make his puny body look bigger so he wears more clothes . . . Jus Ki, Jus Ki."

"You're an asshole Nichols, you're one to talk you scrawny bastard. Jus Ki, Jus Ki . . . besides, I had to wear clothes so yo' mama wouldn't get turned on by my masculine frame 'cause the bitch would probably jump me when I'm trying to turn a double play."

T.J. snuck a remark in from the side even though he was taking batting practice. "The only double play you'd be doing Crook is double playing with your cock because we all know you won't ever get laid." A bunch of he-he's and ha-ha's followed. I laughed along also. We all joked around. We were a close team and if one kid was getting picked on, the whole team would just tear the poor fella apart. Naturally, the trash talking was usually started by one of the E.B. gang members. We were the main instigators, with Jeff at the top of the instigating list.

The coach came back from batting practice, as well as his pre-game talk with the umpire. He tried to get us all in a circle to psyche the team up. He had a husky voice, but quite loud. Of course, he was always screaming so I guess his voice just naturally became loud. He was a small guy and seemed harmless in stature, but he had an intimidating stare to him. He had a mustache and his eyes would just zone in on you when he was mad at you.

"C'mon, C'mon, get in the circle. You guys better get into this game once you get out there. The other team is nothing compared to you and if you straddle around on that field like you did during warm-ups, then you're going to get your asses kicked, I can tell you that now. So let's get into it. C'mon now!"

Jeff was still searching around the bench for his hat and glove. At first, the coach started to zone in on him with that death stare, but then a slight smile protruded from his face. That made me quite happy because I really wasn't in the mood to hear him scream again.

Jeff finally found his hat and glove and stumbled over to our team circle. The coach just looked at him with that mobster type grin and laughed. He muttered some words about "spending half my time baby-sitting that kid. He wins games but puts gray on the head doing it."

I understood where the coach was coming from. Jeff was a unique kid, always losing stuff. You would think he was dumb if you just met him. He was a hell of an athlete though and you just had to love him.

We took our positions on the field and did our usual trash talking and joking around during warm-ups. "Jeff, the ball's coming down, make sure you back me up." I always had to tell him where to be during warm-ups, but during the game, he was always in the right position at the right time.

I distinctly remember one play in that game. Man on first, no outs, tie game, fifth inning, fifth man up to bat. "Hey!" He didn't hear me so I had to scream louder. "Hey Spot!"

After I called him by his nickname, he looked at me with his dumb look. "What?"

"Well, who's got the bag?"

"I don't know."

"Well, you take it . . . it's a right-hander." The second baseman would usually take the bag on a right-hander and the shortstop most often took it on a left-hander, and I decided to stick with the baseball logic.

Jeff just gave me a quick nod and walked back to his position fairly close to the base in case the man on first tried to steal. The pitcher then threw a slow curveball and it was hit to me. It was a pretty hard grounder, one of those that scattered left and then right before finding a groove. I fielded it with ease and made my turn to begin the double play. My trusty buddy Jeff was there waiting at second, catching the ball with a ballet dancer's grace and firing it to first all in the same motion. I could only smile. Jeff and I pulled a lot of those double plays that year. We were a good combination. He smiled back. Then he said, "Easy as yo' mama . . . Jus Ki, Jus Ki." I just laughed and said, "Hey man, that's your business. It's either Corrinne or my mom though, right?"

Everybody knew that Corrinne liked him and always picked on him about it. But he didn't like her as anything more than a friend. He just waved his hands and made a "psst, psst" sound to tell me that there was nothing between them.

I blinked my eyes for the first time because the lamp had been getting too bright for my retina to handle. The lamp was like the fire I had in my eye, a perpetual burning until my hunger and need to forget the pain was satisfied. The letters stood out boldly, spelling out **"BRAVES"**. I turned off the lamp quickly so that darkness could devour my mind and save it from thinking too much. Sometimes, it's bad to think too much. First of all, you start thinking about one topic, and then you think of another and another until your brain can no longer withstand all the information, and you start ruminating in circles. And then you forget what you were even thinking about in the first place.

I hadn't played baseball my freshman year of college. I was more in the mood to hang out with friends and drink my worth of whatever my 138-pound frame could handle. But I did plan to try out in the fall of the next college year. It won't be the same though. I'm sure of that. My buddy won't be there ever again. I'll have no one to scream at during warm-ups, nobody to be aware of what's going on when it counts, nobody to look at me and make a joke about my mom after we both completed an important double play.

The darkness was more of a causal agent to begin my thinking once again rather than a deterrent. I could see nothing but darkness surrounding me, and the only thing left to do was imagine. And so I did. My mind fluttered back to another time in baseball, when Jeff hit a homerun. The ball wavered over the wall with a ferocious swing of the bat, and Jeff took his trot around the bases and the whole team congratulated him as he crossed home. He sat next to me when we came back to the bench and said something to me that will always stick in my mind. "It was weird. It was like I was in a dream world when I was running around those bases." I just stared at him and laughed. The sun was beating down on my neck and I kept blinking my eyes as they filled with dust. I sat there and thought about how great it would be to hit that homerun and be in that dream world.

I turned on the lantern hoping to find some cure for my ruminating mind. I picked it up again and waved it in front of my eyes to bring myself out of my relaxed, drunken stage. Sometimes I felt like an alcoholic; and I could finally understand how one could become an alcoholic. Sometimes it seems as if alcohol is the only thing left that gives you hope, only because it allows you to forget reality for a moment, and give you a vacation from the pain. I drank to pull myself away from reality, but now even drinking wouldn't relieve me of my pain.

The car crash happened on a Thursday and now he's stuck in a nightmare. He was in his dream world, but that dream world turned to reality. Now that he's in his nightmare, I'm not sure if he'll ever come out.

It's amazing how something can change so quickly. It can happen to anybody. I mean, he was a real good kid and it seems unfair for that to happen to him. It makes me realize that I don't have it so rough. He never hurt God; he never hurt anybody. But people say that God works in mysterious ways and all anybody can do is hope and pray that Jeff comes out of his situation, and into the man that he used to be.

I don't want to think of the way he is now. I like to remember the successful athlete and buddy that he was. I remember everything in slow motion. Oh man, did we pull off that double play. And then that smile when he congratulated me. I miss hearing him joke around about my mom. Then I see him slowly turn around, still smiling and the sun shining on his cap. His number eleven casting out brightly, flaunting itself to the spectators. He had that weird walk. His skinny arms far out to his side and his back slightly bent, his long legs always walking in normal strides.

Yeah ... I remember seeing him then ...

... seeing him the way I like to remember him.

<>The way I like to remember him<>